The Princeton

# All

# *U*

# Can

# Eat

# Books in The Princeton Review Series

Cracking the ACT
Cracking the ACT with Sample Tests on CD-ROM
Cracking the CLEP (College-Level Examination Test)
Cracking the GED
Cracking the GMAT
Cracking the GMAT with Sample Tests on Computer Disk
Cracking the GRE
Cracking the GRE with Sample Tests on Computer Disk
Cracking the GRE Biology Subject Test
Cracking the GRE Literature in English Subject Test
Cracking the GRE Psychology Subject Test
Cracking the LSAT
Cracking the LSAT with Sample Tests on Computer Disk
Cracking the LSAT with Sample Tests on CD-ROM
Cracking the MAT (Miller Analogies Test)
Cracking the SAT and PSAT
Cracking the SAT and PSAT with Sample Tests on Computer Disk
Cracking the SAT and PSAT with Sample Tests on CD-ROM
Cracking the SAT II: Biology Subject Test
Cracking the SAT II: Chemistry Subject Test
Cracking the SAT II: English Subject Tests
Cracking the SAT II: French Subject Test
Cracking the SAT II: History Subject Tests
Cracking the SAT II: Math Subject Tests
Cracking the SAT II: Physics Subject Test
Cracking the SAT II: Spanish Subject Test
Cracking the TOEFL with Audiocassette

Flowers & Silver MCAT
Flowers Annotated MCAT
Flowers Annotated MCATs with Sample Tests on Computer Disk
Flowers Annotated MCATs with Sample Tests on CD-ROM

Culturescope Grade School Edition
Culturescope High School Edition
Culturescope College Edition

SAT Math Workout
SAT Verbal Workout

All U Can Eat
Don't Be a Chump!
How to Survive Without Your Parents' Money
Speak Now!
Trashproof Resumes

Biology Smart
Grammar Smart
Math Smart
Reading Smart
Study Smart
Word Smart: Building an Educated Vocabulary
Word Smart II: How to Build a More Educated Vocabulary
Word Smart Executive
Word Smart Genius
Writing Smart

Grammar Smart Junior
Math Smart Junior
Word Smart Junior
Writing Smart Junior

Business School Companion
College Companion
Law School Companion
Medical School Companion

Student Access Guide to College Admissions
Student Advantage Guide to the Best 310 Colleges
Student Advantage Guide to America's Top Internships
Student Advantage Guide to Business Schools
Student Advantage Guide to Law Schools
Student Advantage Guide to Medical Schools
Student Advantage Guide to Paying for College
Student Advantage Guide to Summer
Student Advantage Guide to Visiting College Campuses
Student Advantage Guide: Help Yourself
Student Advantage Guide: The Complete Book of Colleges
Student Advantage Guide: The Internship Bible
Student Advantage Guide to Graduate Schools: Engineering
Hillel Guide to Jewish Life on Campus
International Students' Guide to the United States
The Princeton Review Guide to Your Career

**Also available on cassette from Living Language**
Grammar Smart
Word Smart
Word Smart II

The Princeton Review

# All

# *U*

## Can

## Eat

**Make it *fast!***
**Make it *cheap!***
**Make it *delicious!***

**by Lela Nargi**

with illustrations by
**Adam Hurwitz**

http://www.randomhouse.com     Random House, Inc.     New York   1996

ISBN 0-679-76907-2

Edited by Chris Kensler
Designed by John Bergdahl

Permissions
Excerpt from *Kitchen*, by Banana Yoshimoto, copyright 1988, Grove/Atlantic, Inc. Excerpt from *The Picayune's Creole Cook Book*, copyright 1901, Random House, Inc. Data from "Kitchen Gadgets That Work," by Mark Bittman, 12/6/95, copyright ©1995 by The New York Times Company. Excerpt from *The Food Pharmacy Guide to Good Eating* by Jean Carper. Copyright ©1991 by Jean Carper. Used by permission of Bantam Books, a division of Bantam Doubleday Dell Publishing Group, Inc. Excerpt from *A House In the Country* by Jose Donoso, copyright 1978, Random House, Inc. Excerpt from *Lang's Compendium of Culinary Nonsense and Trivia*, by George Lang. Permission granted by George Lang. Excerpt from *This Boy's Life* by Tobias Wolff, copyright 1989, Grove/Atlantic, Inc. Excerpt from the May, 1995 issue of *The Atlantic Monthly* ©1995.

9  8  7  6  5  4  3  2  1

For Ford

# Acknowledgments

Although the time allotted to the writing of this cookbook was limited, it was time enough to become indebted to hordes of people. Included among the generous and enthusiastic friends to whom I am eternally grateful: Adam Hurwitz, who got me this gig and drew the illustrations; John Bergdahl who designed the book and created the icons; Rob Edwards and Jen Weir, who gave me a home; Louis C.K., John Deckoff, Margo Glass, Pablo Eglysias, and Andy Braum, who subjected themselves to the indignity of my questionable interviewing skills; Alix Bailey and the Bailey clan at large; Lydia Vivante, Dan Havlick, Dan Gorn and Erica Gorn, who wracked their brains for recipes and all-around good ideas; Nick DeLuca at Astor Place Wines & Spirits for his quick but thorough wine lesson; and Chris Kensler, my editor and new friend, for his diligence and good humor.

# Contents

# Introduction: Stop! Don't Go Any Further Until You've Read This

This cookbook is intended for use by precisely the type of person who would never think of buying a cookbook. If you're one of these people, we'll assume that the cookbook-free state of your bookcase cannot be attributed to your staggering brilliance in the kitchen, but rather is due to a conscious decision not to cook. We'll even take a stab at your reasons: You've never cooked before; you tried once and screwed it up; you think it's too complicated, time-consuming, boring, pointless for one person, expensive, messy, etcetera, etcetera . . .

Truth be told, we've all experienced at least some of these misgivings at one time or another, but we got over them pretty quickly because the alternatives to cooking for yourself are: 1. Getting someone else to cook for you (an idle pipe dream?), 2. Eating out, or 3. Ordering in. And doing these things usually means: 1. Going broke, 2. Getting fat, or 3. Consuming things you wouldn't feed your dog, simply because they're cheap and quick.

## The Information Supermarket

For recipes, tips, and food-related laughs, check out these websites:

Yahoo! Entertainment: Food and Eating: Recipes (http://www.yahoo.com/Entertainment/Food-and-Eating/Recipes/) More food-and-humor-stuffed home pages than you can shake kabob at.

The Burrito Page (http://www.infobahn.com/pages/rito.html) Try your hand at the great recipes on this website and take the Burrito Toppings Personality Quiz.

Catherine's Recipe of the Week (http://www.glob-alserve.on.ca/-cbar-rett/previous.html) Check this website out for easy-to-prepare meals.

We'll make a little confession to you right up front: No one involved in putting this cookbook together is a professionally trained chef. We learned to cook by sitting in the kitchen while our relatives were doing it, by watching Julia Child on cable, by reading cookbooks, by preparing dozens of disastrous meals, and by sheer force of will. Why? Because we always thought the idea of cooking was pretty cool (even when we were completely baffled as to how to go about it), and because we like to show off in front of our friends. What we're really saying is: If we can do it, so can you.

There are two things we believe about cooking, and we want you to believe them, too: Cooking is easy, and cooking is fun. This book has been compiled with these basic premises in mind. Every dish in here is something we eat ourselves with regularity and, above all, something we enjoy eating. Hopefully, you will, too.

We've tried to cover all the bases in this book. Chapter 1 is a primer on cooking utensils and appliances. It's really meant to provide you with some guidelines, but there's no reason why you can't cook a meal for yourself even if you don't own all the utensils we've listed—it's absolutely fine if you only have one big pot, one frying pan, a sharp knife, and a can opener. Buy more utensils when you have the money or feel the need. Exercise a little common sense (i.e., don't try to fit four cups of liquid into a pot that holds 12 ounces), and you'll do just fine. The first chapter also contains a few how-to's we hope you'll find useful, like how to light the oven and how to defrost your freezer.

The purpose of chapter 2 is to see you through your first solitary trip to the supermarket. We've second-guessed you a bit by imagining what items you think you'll need to have in your cabinets, but if you know for a fact you'll never use honey, then of course don't buy it. We've also given you some tips on storage and shelf life.

Chapter 3 gets a little closer to the kitchen. If you've never used a kitchen before, it *is* plausible that you don't know how to boil water or chop an onion, so don't be embarrassed. We're here to help.

Chapters 4 through 11 are all recipe chapters. Again, we've tried to cover all the bases, with lots of different ways to cook basic dishes, spice up prepared foods, and throw a party. Each recipe has a header indicating how long it takes to prepare, how many people it serves, how hard it is to make (ranging from 1 for easy to 3 for difficult), whether or not it's spicy, and ways you can make it a little fancier.

Whatever recipe you choose to prepare, we recommend you read it thoroughly first to make sure you have all the ingredients and that you know what you're getting yourself into. And please don't be put off by recipes that look long. Often, a recipe is long by virtue of the number of spices it contains, or because it has a lot of steps that mostly instruct you to do easy things like chopping, or adding salt to boiling water.

## Key to Icons

 Level of Difficulty

 Number of Servings

 Preparation Time

 Spicy

 Getting Fancy

 What to Read

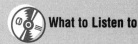 What to Listen to

## Magazines

For recipes, tips, and uncanny food phenomena, peruse these journals in your local magazine rack:

*Cook's Illustrated* has an elegant cover and a piquant approach to food advice.
To subscribe: Write Cook's Illustrated, P.O. Box 7444, Red Oak, LA 51591-0444.

*Eating Well: The Magazine of Food and Health* is full of nutritional information and uncomplicated, gourmet recipes for the health-conscious to try.
To subscribe: Call 1 (800) 678-0541.

*Cooking Light: The Magazine of Food and Fitness* presents dozens of light recipes per issue.
To subscribe: Call 1 (800) 336-0125.

*Food and Wine* is the bible of both.
To subscribe: Call 1 (800) 333-6569.

Cooking is not an exact science, and it often benefits from improvisation. As you get more used to cooking, don't be so concerned with following recipes to the letter. Obviously, you can always add salt, pepper, and hot spices to taste rather than following our suggestions. If you think it's a good idea to add Tabasco to meatloaf, or pineapple to pancakes, try it and see what happens.

We want you to outgrow this cookbook. The reason we've added "Getting Fancy" at the end of many recipes is so you'll be encouraged to experiment, and learn something about cooking in the process. And as you go along, you may find yourself wanting to know more about, say, Indian or vegetarian cooking, which is why you'll find "What to Read" sidebars in every chapter. We also suggest various songs and albums with cooking and food themes. Good kitchen music is key to good cooking (plus we can't help imposing our musical tastes on you, the unsuspecting public). Finally: Don't be afraid to mess up this cookbook. The more stuck together the pages are with sauce and oil and assorted cooking gunk, the more you're using the book, and the more flattered we'll be.

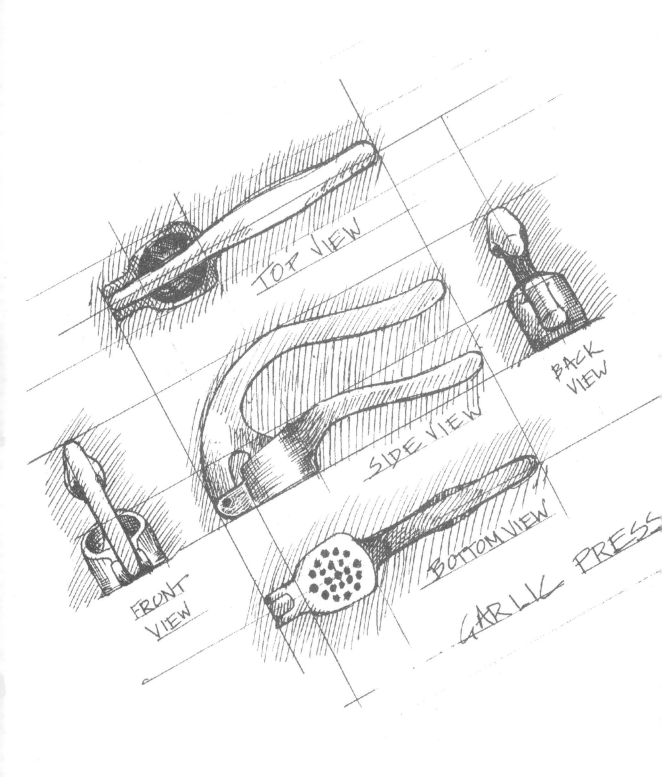

TOP VIEW

BACK VIEW

SIDE VIEW

FRONT VIEW

BOTTOM VIEW

GARLIC PRESS

# 1

# *The Basics: Equipping Your Kitchen*

## Common Kitchen Implements and You

You've seen all these things before: in your parents' kitchen, on TV, in that childhood nightmare where all the appliances came to life and tried to force you to eat liver. You never thought the day would come when you would have any use for these contraptions. But, surprise, surprise . . . here you are with your own kitchen and no clue how to get it to make you a meal. Well, today must be your lucky day, because we know and we're going to tell you. We're even going to draw you a few pictures.

# Things that Go on the Stove and in the Oven

### The baking sheet

If you ever want to make cookies, this is the item for you. It comes in regular and nonstick.

### The roasting pan

Ribs, roasts, birds, butts — the roasting pan holds them all. If you don't feel like dropping the cash on the real thing, purchase disposable aluminum pans at the supermarket instead (also recommended for people who hate doing dishes).

### The roasting rack

This ingenious little item is made of metal slats and fits snugly into a roasting pan. If you hate the idea of the bottom of your chicken or pot roast getting all soggy, you're going to thank your lucky stars you had the foresight to purchase one of these.

### The saucepot

Perfect for cooking frozen vegetables, making rice, and heating up soup. Ideally, it comes with a lid.

### The skillet

Yes, it looks pretty much like a frying pan, but usually it's made out of some heavy metal, like cast iron. You can use it to fry up just about anything: hamburgers (p. 119), pancakes (p. 55), stir-fry (p. 159), leftovers. If you're only going to buy one frying pan, the skillet is the way to go. Because it's so heavy, it distributes heat more evenly than a cheap aluminum pan, and you'll be amazed at how hard a time you'll have trying to burn something.

## The stockpot

This is a big pot with a handle on either side toward the top. It comes in a variety of sizes: 6-quart, 8-quart, 10-quart, and 12-quart. The smallest stockpot is ideal for making chili (p. 194), stew (p. 126), or a single serving of spaghetti. Use the larger stockpot for cooking a big wad of pasta, or for boiling lasagna noodles. A 12-quart's invaluable when your roof springs a leak during a heavy rainstorm.

## The wok

As with the cast iron skillet, you can fry up just about anything in a wok, and fry it up quick. Stir-fry (p. 159), sausage with tomato and onion (p. 134), curry (pp. 137, 156)—you can make all these and so much more. Steak and burgers, however, are a bit more of a challenge.

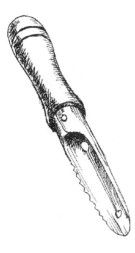

# Things with Handles

## The apple corer

This looks kind of like a peeler with a moon-shaped, serrated edge. You probably won't use it that often but, hey, it only costs about two bucks and it'll make your life a lot easier when you try our recipe for baked apples (p.174). It also doubles as an awkward peeler.

## The can opener

You know how this works, and if you've ever tried to open a can of tuna without one, you know how desperately you need it. The cheap metal ones work fine, but you do risk having your fingers cramp up. So, splurge on one of the big ones with rubber-coated handles. Electric openers are even pricier, but are fun for the whole family.

## The chef's knife

This is a large knife with a blade that's wide on the handle end and tapers to a point. If you're serious about mastering the art of vegetable chopping, this knife is a must-have. It's also great for hacking up meat and threatening your roommates when they refuse to clean their hair out of the clogged bathtub drain.

## The garlic press

You like guacamole (p. 187)? You want this. No way do you want to risk lopping off a finger to get that garlic chopped fine.

## The grater

The name is self-explanatory: it grates. Use the side with the big holes for grating carrots or cheddar cheese; the side with the little holes for grating fresh Parmesan cheese over spaghetti, or ginger and garlic when you're too lazy to chop them really small with a knife. Just watch your knuckles. And a note to the exceedingly lazy: we've also been known to use it for draining spaghetti when the colander was lodged at the bottom of a cold, water-filled sink of dirty dishes that took six days to accumulate — no way we're sticking our hands in there.

## The knife sharpener

If you've gone ahead and invested a chunk of change into some decent knives, you're going to need one of these. The cheapest knife sharpeners are small, double-sided plastic disks that have the sharpening stone wedged into the center; they barely work, so don't waste your money. Instead, buy one of those knife sharpeners that looks like a giant ice pick, and be prepared to sharpen your knives about once a month, depending on how often you use them. A well-sharpened knife should be able to slice a sheet of paper, dangled from your fingers, neatly in half.

## New York Starters

"I lived on the Upper West Side of New York City and didn't have any cooking stuff at all, just a fork I stole from a friend. I would get a pack of turkey hot dogs for a dollar, and a can of no-name corn that cost, like, twenty-five cents. I opened the corn with a big hunting knife I had; I could have bought a can opener, but I started getting off on the lifestyle. I'd cook the corn in the can on the stove and eat it; then I'd wash out the can and fill it with water and I would boil two hot dogs in it lengthwise. I would eat the hot dogs and then I would clean out the can again and I would make tea in it, and that was my meal for the day. But pretty soon I realized, you know, I had enough money to buy a pan."

by Louis C.K.,
School of Life

## The ladle

Extremely effective in minimizing soup slop when you want to transfer liquid from pot to bowl.

## The paring knife

Essentially, this is just a sharp knife with a short blade and a little handle. Real chefs use it to peel things like potatoes and to carve fancy designs into radishes. You can use it to cut up onions, slice the fat off pork chops, or open the cellophane on a package of ramen noodles. Also handy for taking the skin off apples and pears.

## The peeler

No mystery here, either. Potatoes, carrots, cucumbers — if it's got skin you don't want to eat, this'll get rid of it. A safety tip: always peel away from your body.

## The potato masher

Just trust us on this: you want one. Works like a charm.

## The slotted spoon

When you're too lazy to find the pot holders to drain the boiled potatoes into the colander, the slotted spoon will save your butt. This brilliant invention enables you to fish the potatoes, or the frozen peas, or the ravioli, right out of the hot water without scalding your fingers.

## The spatula

Just try to make an omelet (p. 53) without one. Or french toast (p. 56). Or grilled cheese (p. 68). Metal is the sturdiest and most durable; plastic is essential if your frying pan is Teflon-coated.

## The whisk

It performs the function of a glorified fork and, like the stockpot, comes in many handy sizes. The smallest works well for stirring salad dressing (p. 82), the medium, for beating eggs, combining pancake batter (p. 55), and mixing the ingredients for banana bread (p. 177). The large one is totally useless unless you want all your friends to think you're some sort of kitchen wizard, in which case it should be displayed prominently above the stove.

# Bowls with Holes

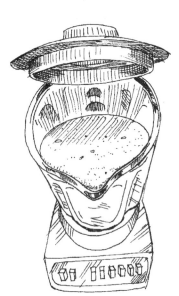

## The colander

Commonly referred to as the "spaghetti drainer," this bowl-shaped implement with holes in the bottom is ideal for just that. But the fun just begins there: Use it to drain canned tuna fish or tomatoes, boiled potatoes and other vegetables, you name it. Use it to wash lettuce, spinach, fresh herbs, anything leafy. A little-known fact: it's great for steaming vegetables (p. 45), and for heating up leftover Chinese dumplings.

## The sieve

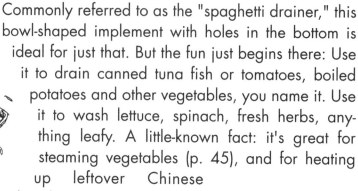

Like the colander, the sieve is useful for draining things. Made out of mesh and sporting a long handle, it can also be used to sift flour when you bake, and for evenly dusting a waffle with powdered sugar.

# Plug it In

## The blender

Don't believe the hype about the food processor being the most important kitchen machine in the universe. Who's got $200 to drop on a plastic contraption with a blade that's just going to take up valuable counter space and can't even make a milk

shake? Reasonably priced at about $40, the blender can make a milk shake, as well as pureed soups and all manner of mashed vegetables, for when you have your wisdom teeth extracted and need to suck down all your meals through a straw.

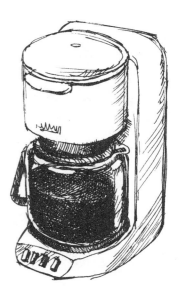

## The coffee/espresso pot

There are two ways to produce a cup of coffee: in an electric coffee maker or over a mug with a plastic filter-holder. Likewise, there are two ways to make espresso: the electric way and the stovetop way, with one of those cute little pots. Your finances will determine which method is for you.

## The hand mixer

In all fairness, this is not an essential item, though we couldn't imagine living without one. Then again, we like to bake, and the hand mixer makes whipping up batter a cinch.

## The hot pot

An all-time classic. Anything liquid can be heated up in this: water for tea, canned soup and, of course, ramen noodles (pp. 110-113).

## Nuking It

Have you ever wondered how microwaves work? The principle behind them was discovered during World War II, when army technicians noticed that rations left near radar gear warmed up. The radio waves emitted by microwave ovens are tuned to the natural frequency of the water molecules present in food and cause them to vibrate (heat up). This is why it is difficult to make roasts or similarly complex dishes in a microwave: the temperature of the food rarely rises above 212 degrees fahrenheit, the temperature at which water turns to steam. This isn't quite hot enough to roast most meats. So, while some cooks still swear that the microwave could replace the conventional oven entirely, it hasn't done so to anywhere near the extent that manufacturers predicted it would in the mid-1980s. Indeed, in many households, the microwave acts as a $200 popcorn popper.

## The microwave

If your parents gave you one, great; if not, don't fret. Microwaves aren't all they're cracked up to be. They can't even boil water. However, they are extremely useful for heating up leftovers, thawing items that you forgot to remove from the freezer before school or work, and cooking frozen dinners. Warning: They mean what they say about no metal.

## The toaster oven

God forbid you should live in an apartment that has no oven, but if you do, the toaster oven is invaluable for heating up frozen dinners, making toast, baking potatoes, puffing up pitas . . . you get the picture. Advertisements for some models display a whole chicken roasting contentedly inside, but we're not convinced.

# Miscellaneous

## The measuring cup

Usually made out of heat-proof Pyrex, and designed to measure up to eight ounces.

## Measuring spoons

Made out of plastic or metal; four spoons measure 1/2 teaspoon, 1 teaspoon, 1/2 tablespoon, and 1 tablespoon.

## Plastic Tupperware containers

A real money saver. Not only do they extend the life of your leftovers, allowing you to get two, or even three, meals out of one cooking experiment, but you won't waste expensive aluminum foil and Saran Wrap covering up your leftovers in bowls.

# Less Common Kitchen Implements and Why You'll Never Need Them

It was really sweet of Aunt Betty to retrieve that box of kitchen stuff from the attic and give it to you as a house-warming gift, but what use do you have for an electric skillet? If you're doing things right, absolutely none. Ditto for the mushroom brush, the garlic roaster, and the shrimp deveiner (yes, there really is such a thing). Below, even more stuff you can live without.

## Crêpe pan

What are you, some kind of showoff? We're not even going to tell you how to make crêpes, so there.

## Space-Age Kitchen

A shrimp deveiner isn't the only thing you don't need in your kitchen. Below, a few items taken from the Hammacher Schlemmer catalog, which could easily fall into a "Most Useless but Still Somehow Appealing" category.

1. Message-Making Toaster: Prints a message—like "Happy Birthday" or "Good Morning"—right onto your toast.

2. Pop-Up Hot Dog Cooker: Two hot dogs and two buns are inserted into a contraption that looks and works like a toaster.

3. Electric Home Snowcone Machine: Comes with two packages of pre-sweetened Kool Aid, to help you recapture the sugar fits of your youth.

## Egg slicer

When was the last time you ate a sliced egg?

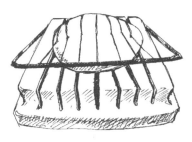

## Electric steamer

Why bother? Get a colander.

## Fish poacher

Poached fish? If you must poach, use your dishwasher (p. 144).

## Grapefruit spoon

You could put someone's eye out with that thing.

## Jar opener

It looks like a clever idea, but you risk straining muscles you never knew you had. The old running-the-lid-under-hot-water-then-banging-it-senseless-against-the-counter-top method is still effective.

## Lemon zester

If you really, really want lemon zest, you can get the same results using a grater. If you don't know what lemon zest is, you won't want this anyway.

## Pasta measurer

All you need to know is that 1/4 box (that is, 1/4 pound, usually) of spaghetti equals one serving.

## Poultry scissors

Do you really want to spend 45 minutes cutting slimy chicken skin off the carcass? Better to save yourself the effort and just ingest it (cooked, of course).

## Salad spinner

Yes, dry lettuce is a good idea (wet lettuce doesn't hold salad dressing), but you can get most of the excess water off by shaking it in a colander, and the rest by wrapping it in a dish towel.

## Turkey baster

Just use a spoon.

# The Major Appliances

Your kitchen's got a stove and a refrigerator, but do you have any idea how to use them?

## The stove

There are two kinds of stoves: gas and electric. If the burners are flat metal disks, it's electric and it'll take a few minutes for them to get warmed up once you've turned them on. They don't heat things as quickly as gas, so be prepared to increase the cooking times in recipes.

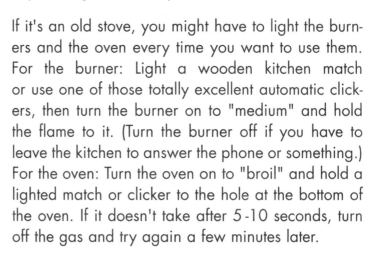

New gas stoves usually have a safety feature requiring that you push the knob in, then turn it counterclockwise to "light." If you can't get the burners lit, first check to see if the pilot light has gone out by lifting up the whole top of the stove; there should be two small flames, one on either side of the stove. If they're not lit, try and get your Super to light them for you.

If it's an old stove, you might have to light the burners and the oven every time you want to use them. For the burner: Light a wooden kitchen match or use one of those totally excellent automatic clickers, then turn the burner on to "medium" and hold the flame to it. (Turn the burner off if you have to leave the kitchen to answer the phone or something.) For the oven: Turn the oven on to "broil" and hold a lighted match or clicker to the hole at the bottom of the oven. If it doesn't take after 5-10 seconds, turn off the gas and try again a few minutes later.

## The refrigerator

Every refrigerator has a dial inside by the light for adjusting the temperature. "Five" is usually standard, but if your leftovers are turning to solid blocks of ice, turn the setting down to "Three" or "Four." Obviously, if nothing's getting cold, turn the setting up a bit.

If you don't have a frost-free freezer, the day will eventually come when you have to spend six hours at the unpleasant task of defrosting. You'll know this day has arrived when you can no longer shut the freezer door or when there's no room inside for a tray of ice. This is the also the optimum time to throw out old food, wipe off the shelves, and wash that gelatinous brown sludge out of the vegetable drawer.

To defrost: Take every single thing out of the fridge. Throw away leftovers and moldy food, and put frozen items and anything severely perishable into a big, clean bucket and cover it all with whatever ice cubes you have in your freezer. Turn the temperature setting to "Off" or "Defrost," and use a piece of duct tape to hold down the button that keeps the light on. If your freezer has become too small with ice build-up to hold a saucepot, boil up a big stockpot of water and place it on the top shelf of the refrigerator and close the door almost all the way.

Otherwise, boil a saucepot of water and put it in the freezer, close the freezer door, and leave the refrigerator door ajar. Re-boil the water and replace it in the freezer or fridge every time it cools. Believe us, this will take hours.

As the ice begins to melt, water will accumulate in the drawer under the freezer. To prevent it from overflowing, every time you reheat your pot of water, remove the drawer, empty it, and replace. After a while, big blocks of ice will start falling off. Toss them in the sink.

The only pleasurable thing about the whole defrosting event is that it gives you a chance to vent your aggression: a heavy, blunt instrument (a knife sharpener's perfect; a hammer works, too) can be used to take exceedingly satisfying whacks at the ice blocks that aren't melting fast enough. Don't use anything sharp for this—you don't want to burst the Freon pipes—and try to avoid hitting parts of the freezer that are no longer ice-bound. Also, you might want to put a large towel on the floor in front of the fridge to alleviate some of the flooding.

After you've wasted a whole afternoon doing this, your freezer should be totally ice-free. Empty the drawer of water for the last time, clean out the inside of the fridge with Windex or Fantastic or whatever cleaning product you have, then turn the temperature setting back on, remove the tape that's keeping the light off, and put all of your food back in the fridge.

# 2

# *The Aisles Have It: Shopping at the Supermarket*

## Buying and Storing the Basics

### Staples first

To properly stock your kitchen, there are some basics you absolutely can't do without. We've compiled a list of everything we could think of that you'll need to get started, along with a notation on where and how long to store it. The list may look huge, but unless you want to spend half an hour in the supermarket every day, what with those long lines, surly cashiers, and old fogies blocking the aisles with their carts, one-time kamikaze shopping for all your basics is the least-stressful option. Also, it's not like you're going

to be picking up things like oil and salt with too much regularity anyway, so what you spend your first time out is not indicative of what you'll be spending on your weekly visits.

# Products from a Cow's Udder

## Cream cheese

Check the date on the box to make sure you've got at least two months, then store it in the fridge. Throw it away when it turns blue.

## Other cheeses (Cheddar, Swiss, American, etc.)

Storage and date-checking is the same as for cream cheese. Those Kraft singles will keep almost forever, mostly because they're individually wrapped. Blocks of cheese need to be meticulously rewrapped in Saran Wrap or they'll get dark and hard where the air hits them. Most cheeses, you should know, taste better if you let them warm to room temperature before you eat them.

## Butter/Margarine

Keep the sticks you're using in the refrigerator; keep the sticks you're not using in the freezer. Same goes for tubs. Always keep a stick-in-use (or a tub-in-use) covered. For sticks, you can use the paper wrapper; tubs come with nifty lids for just this purpose. You'll probably use your butter or margarine quick enough so that you won't have to worry about spoilage, but get rid of the frozen stuff after three months, the refrigerated stuff after three weeks.

## Milk

Keep it in the refrigerator on that handy door shelf. Always check the date on top of the carton to make sure you've got at least a week's leeway. Whole milk lasts longest because of the fat content, skim spoils quickest. The sniff test is still the best indicator of freshness once you've opened the carton: If it has any odor at all, chuck it. Don't even bother to smell it if you can hear clumps rattling around when you shake the carton.

## Parmesan cheese

The same as other cheeses unless you buy the pre-grated, jarred stuff. Check the date.

# Products from a Fertile Chicken

## Eggs

Store them in the fridge, but not in those oh-so-appealing-built-in egg holders. Eggs will last up to a month if kept in the carton. If the egg doesn't just plop right out of the shell when you crack it open, don't use it.

# Products from Grains

## Sliced bread

There are a couple of ways you can go here. If you plan to use the whole package, untoasted, within five days, keep it in the refrigerator or on top of it,

## Yin/Yang

For thousands of years, the Chinese have believed that an individual's wellbeing is affected by the yin/yang balance, which is directly influenced by diet. The trick is not to depend too heavily on either side of the balance for your nutrition.

Yin foods: raw fruits and vegetables; cold-water fish

Yin spices: salt; soy sauce

Yang foods: meats, such as chicken, pork, and lamb

Yang spices: garlic; ginger; black pepper

Neutral foods: rice; bread

## Under the Weather?

Feeling under the weather? Bypass the medicine cabinet and head straight for your spice rack. Munch a little thyme to alleviate symptoms of the common cold; nibble some anise to cure gas pains; graze your way through a bunch of basil to dispel nausea; and for heartburn, try chomping a sprig of peppermint.

(Source: *The Food Pharmacy Guide to Good Eating*, by Jean Carper)

depending on your bug situation (remember to reseal the bag). If you want it just for toast or for the occasional sandwich, keep it in the freezer and take out slices as you want them. Again, check the freshness date on the plastic closure. Keep in mind that, well-sealed, the loaf will keep for months in the freezer; out of it, it'll go stale or moldy pretty soon after the date on the package. The same goes for pitas. And if you're into preservative-free breads, the risk is all yours.

# Products that Are Very, Very Cold

## Frozen vegetables

Store them in the freezer for up to three months. Cooked, store in plastic in the fridge for up to five days.

## Orange juice

Both the cartons and the frozen containers have dates stamped on them; let these be your guide. Keep the frozen stuff in the freezer until you mix it up, then in the fridge, covered. Keep the cartons in the fridge.

# Products that Are Dry

## Baking powder

Store in the cabinet. Check the date or risk unleavened pancakes.

# Baking soda

All those commercials are true: an open box of baking soda really does absorb all those nasty refrigerator odors. If you plan to bake, keep a second box in a ziplock bag in the cabinet. Check the expiration date.

# Bisquick

Store for up to a year in the cabinet.

# Bouillon cubes

Store indefinitely in the cabinet or on the spice rack. Note: Recipes in this book that call for one bouillon cube do so with the assumption that the cube is meant to be reconstituted to one cup. Knorr, however, makes double-sized cubes (that is, meant to reconstitute to two cups). Make sure you know which one you've got, or you could really be packing in the MSG.

# Cereal

Store it in the cabinet for up to a month once it's opened, and remember to close the bag well so the contents don't go stale.

# Flour

Maybe it's just wishful thinking on our part, but we think flour stays fresher if you keep the open bag in the fridge, not that we've ever encountered rotten flour. You can also prevent most flour-related messes by storing it in a glass or plastic canister with a wide mouth for easy spoon or measuring cup insertion. If there's no room in the fridge and you're too lazy to put it in a canister, keep an open bag of flour in a big ziplock bag in the cabinet.

## Macaroni & Cheese

See "Pasta." Once it's all cooked up, leftovers can be stored in the refrigerator in a plastic container, or in a bowl under Saran Wrap. Leftovers taste infinitely less cheesy than fresh.

## Pasta

Keeps close to forever, with the box open or closed (actually, recommended storage time is up to a year). Keep in the cabinet unless you have bugs, in which case keep it in the fridge.

## Ramen noodles

See "Pasta." Leftovers can be stored in the fridge for a couple of days.

## Rice

Store in the cabinet for up to a year. Don't bother saving leftovers, which get hard almost instantly. Minute rice is totally devoid of nutrients, so try not to buy it. Carolina long-grain rice is our brand of choice, but buy brown if it's something you can stomach, basmati if you're interested in a bit of a taste and texture change and have been experimenting with Indian cooking, and wild rice if you've got some extra dollars to blow.

## Sugar

Store the box in the cabinet, or empty contents into a sugar bowl, jar, or dispenser and keep on your countertop.

# Products that Come in Cans or Jars

## Canned soup

Keep it in the cabinet. Otherwise, follow directions as for canned tomatoes.

## Canned tomatoes

Infinite cabinet life unopened. If you use only a fraction of the can, store the remainder in a covered plastic container in the fridge because opened cans tend to get moldy around the rim. Opened canned tomatoes will keep about a week, or a week-and-a-half stored in this way. White film floating on the top is a good indicator that it's time to toss them out.

## Spaghetti sauce

Lasts a mighty long time in the cabinet until you open it, then lasts about a week-and-a-half in the fridge.

## Tuna

Unopened, lasts forever and ever. Keep leftovers in the fridge in plastic containers (including leftover tuna salads) for no more than three days.

## Mushrooms

These are the types of mushroom you're most likely to find at your grocery store. While white mushrooms are the norm, try some of the other types in your recipes, and see what happens.

Cultivated white mushroom: Mild, earthy flavor; "buttons" are the youngest of these.

Cremino: Dark brown variety of white mushroom; fuller flavor; also referred to as "common brown" and "Roman."

Portobello: Fully mature form of that same old white mushroom.

Black trumpet: Distinctly horn-shaped; thin; brittle flesh; aromatic with an elegant, buttery flavor.

Hen-of-the-woods: Dark brown to gray; resembles a tightly ruffled puff edged in white.

Matsutake: Dark brown Japanese mushroom; dense, meaty texture; nutty flavor; cooked in numerous ways.

# Products You Can Spread

## Jelly

Keeps for months unopened in the cabinet, months more opened in the fridge. When it goes bad, it will start to crystallize (jelly should never be crunchy), and turn moldy.

## Peanut butter

Open and unopened can be kept in the cabinet; just make sure it's re-sealed all the way. Shelf life is about six months but the rule is, if it looks good, tastes good, and smells good, eat it.

## Mayonnaise

Unopened, the jar will last in the cabinet for a long time. Open, in the fridge, it seems to last just as long. After about a year, it will probably start to discolor slightly. Toss it when that time comes.

## Mustard

See "Mayonnaise."

# Products that Were Picked

## Garlic

Look for heads that are firm and have the outer skin intact.

## Lemons

Give them a good week-and-a-half in the fridge, uncut. Cover with Saran Wrap once you've taken off a slice, then toss after a couple of days. The skin starts to brown when they're fading.

## Lettuce

We are of two minds on the issue of storing lettuce, which doesn't keep very long. The lazy slob in us argues that it stores just fine when kept in a plastic bag in the crisper. On our more neurotic days, we buy a head of lettuce, remove all the leaves, wash them, drain them, wrap them in paper towels, and place them in a ziplock bag in the produce drawer. How anal are you? Only you can say.

## Mushrooms

Store in the produce drawer. After opening, be sure to seal package well with Saran Wrap. Unopened or opened-and-sealed, they should keep for about a week.

## Onions

Store like potatoes. They'll start to sprout as they age (still salvageable, but don't buy them this way). When they're really going bad, they'll be soft.

## Potatoes

Store in the refrigerator produce drawer. They may last for about a month before they start to grow those little green sprouts, a month-and-a-half before they start to shrivel. They're still able to be revived in the sprout stage; hopeless once the skins are less than taut.

Nameko: Small Japanese mushroom; ranges from orange to amber to gold; soft gelantinous texture; rich, earthy aroma and flavor; used often in soups and one-pot dishes.

Oyster: Fan-shaped; pale gray to dark-brown gray; robust and slightly peppery flavor; young ones are the tastiest.

Pom pom: Beautiful, white mushroom; looks like a cheerleader's pompom; firm yet feathery; should not be purchased unless bright white.

Straw: Perfect for Asian dishes; tiny and conical like the hats of paddy workers; pale tan to dark gray; also known as "paddy straw" and "grass" (named after their growing environment: the grasses and straws of a drying paddy field).

Trompette de la mort (trumpet of death): looks like a trumpet; thin cap and gently ruffled; dark gray to black; rich, deep, and nutty flavor.

# Products You Steep

## Coffee

Keep the unopened can in the cabinet, the opened can in the fridge or freezer. Lasts, open, for about a month. Brewed coffee will keep in the fridge for about two days.

## Tea

Keep it in the cabinet. It will eventually lose some flavor, but it won't actually go bad.

# Products in Bottles

## Oil

Ideally, you should have two kinds of oil: vegetable for frying things, and olive if you make salad dressing or spaghetti sauce. Store whatever kind of oil you buy in the cabinet, and keep the top screwed on. If you use oil often, don't worry about it going rancid— it'll take about six months — but keep it away from heat (i.e., the stove), or you'll just be tempting fate.

## Salad dressing

An unopened bottle can go in the cabinet, but some of the fancier brands have freshness dates, so don't forget to check. Keep the open bottle in the refrigerator. If you eat salad a couple of times a week, you'll use the dressing often enough so that you don't have to worry about it going bad.

## Soy sauce

Store it, indefinitely, in the cabinet.

## Tabasco

See "Soy sauce."

## Worcestershire sauce

See "Soy sauce."

## Vinegar

Store it like oil. The best kinds to buy are red wine and balsamic. Avoid white, which is useful only for cleaning coffee pots and reviving leather products.

# Products You Sprinkle on Other Products

## Dried oregano

Keep it in the cabinet, or on the spice rack, but away from the stove; heat makes spices lose their flavor more quickly. Technically, dried spices will keep forever but, like tea, they start to lose flavor after about three months. Same goes for dried basil.

## Garlic powder

See "Dried oregano."

### How to Test a Shopping Cart

They look innocent enough, all those wire carts pushed neatly together near the supermarket entrance. But beware: In every pack there lurks the cart from hell—the one whose wheels will suddenly lock up without warning, causing you to surge painfully forward, stomach first, into the all-too-sturdy handle. To avoid this and other cart-related injuries, there are a few hell-cart indicators you should be on the lookout for. When you pull the prospective vehicle from its nesting place, do the wheels squeak? Does one wheel twitch sideways or not quite touch the ground? To propel the cart forward, are you exerting more effort than would be required to, say, hurl a coffee mug across your apartment at your roommate? If the answer to any of these questions is "yes," abandon the cart and repeat this testing procedure until the cart of your dreams is secured.

## Salt of the Earth

Think plain old table salt exists solely for the purpose of making pretzels palatable? Think again:

1. After you've dyed your clothes the old-fashioned way—that is, with beets—you're going to need something to turn the skin on your fingers back to it's original pallor. That something is salt.

2. Did careless guests spill red wine all over your white shag carpet? Pour on mounds of table salt to soak up the mess.

3. Are you unlucky? Hexed? Downright doomed? Toss a little table salt over your shoulder, sit back, and just wait for the tide of your fortunes to turn.

## Pepper

See "Dried oregano." Same goes for peppercorns, which are preferable to previously ground pepper in terms of flavor. Buy these if someone's given you a pepper mill.

## Salt

Keep the box in the cabinet; add a palmful of raw rice to the salt in your salt shaker to keep it from sticking together. Salt never goes bad.

# Products You Need but Shouldn't Eat

### Brillo pads

Once they get wet, they rust. Keep the box under the sink and the pad-in-use away from big pools of water. Toss it when it turns brown.

### Coffee filters

Store them in the cabinet. They last forever.

### Dish detergent

Bargain brands suck: no grease-cutting power. Get yourself a nice, big bottle of the expensive stuff and keep it on the sink, next to the sponges.

### Fantastic

Keep it under the sink. The other brand of choice is Lysol Direct.

## Garbage bags

If you hate taking the garbage out and don't mind the faint aroma of sewage, buy big garbage bags instead of using those tiny plastic things your groceries come in. Splurge a little on name-brand bags so they won't split and spill rancid vegetables onto your floor when you carry out the refuse. Store them under the sink.

## Paper towels

Do yourself a favor and hook up a paper towel rack.

## Roach/Ant bait

You got bugs? You need bait. Open up the box and scatter the bait around your kitchen according to the directions. Bait usually needs to be replaced every three months.

## Saran Wrap

Keep in the kitchen drawer or under the sink. And try to keep the box intact, otherwise it'll be a bitch to cut off a piece. Name brands are noticeably clingier than bargain.

## Sponges

Keep one on the sink, the others under it. It's also helpful to have one for washing dishes, and another for cleaning the stove and counters.

## Tin foil

It's okay to go for the bargain brands here; no one's figured out how to ruin tin foil yet. Store like Saran Wrap.

## Ziplock bags

See "Tin foil."

# Shopping for the Week

You've got all your staples, but you want a real dinner at least twice a week — you can only eat so many peanut butter sandwiches, right? Every once in a while, you need a big, juicy steak (p. 128) or, if you don't eat meat, a nice stir-fry (p. 159) that contains vegetables picked some time within the last year. Either you can sit down and plan a menu for the week so you only have to make one trip to the supermarket, or you can wait until dinner time rolls around, decide there's no way you're going to eat another peanut butter sandwich, and hightail it down to the store at the last minute to pick up a chicken. The choice is yours.

Below is a list of everything else we could think of that you might want to buy — at the last minute or well in advance — and tips for storing.

# Fresh vegetables

Carrots and celery last a couple of weeks, kept in their cellophane bags in the vegetable drawer of your refrigerator. They're still okay when they start to wilt, but once carrots have shriveled and celery starts to look anemic, it's time to toss them out. Broccoli, peas, cauliflower, zucchini, and peppers last up to a week in plastic bags, but throw them away once they get spotty. Spinach, arugula, and other leafy vegetables last only about three days; their lives may be extended if they're stored like lettuce (p. 29). Try to buy avocados when they're already pretty soft and eat them within two days; otherwise, buy them a little harder and let them ripen on top of the refrigerator. The same goes for tomatoes.

# Fresh fruit

All citrus should be stored in the refrigerator. Other fruit can be left out, but will last longer (maybe a week, if you're lucky) in the fridge. Berries look nasty after about two days, so plan to eat them right away if you buy them.

# Fresh herbs

Parsley, sage, oregano, marjoram, basil: Wash first then keep dry in plastic bags in the crisper. It's okay to use them once they start drying a bit, but if you still have a lot left and hate the idea of throwing them out, remove them from the refrigerator, let them dry completely, then store them in jars or plastic containers, and use them like store-bought dried herbs. Thyme, rosemary: Store and dry them like other

## How to Buy and Store Produce

Grapes: Store grapes in pierced plastic bags in the refrigerator. Do not wash them first; the dusty residue is a protective layer. Wash them just before eating instead.

Peaches, nectarines, and plums: If the fruit is hard, store in a loosely closed paper bag at room temperature until it gives slightly near the stem.

Pears: These too should give slightly near the stem. Check the base too. If it's soft, the pear is probably overripe.

Tomatoes: The redder, the better. Splurge on the greenhouse product for eating raw; get plain plum tomatoes for cooking. Until ripe, store at room temperature. If you can't use them right away when they're ripe, move them to the refrigerator and store stem down, which makes them soften more slowly.

*Mastering the Art of French Cooking Vol. I,* by Julia Child with Louisette Bertholle and Simone Beck, and *Vol. II,* by Julia Child and Simon Beck

*French Cooking for Beginners,* by Helene Siegel

herbs, but don't bother washing them first. Since they're of hardier stock, they'll probably last in the fridge for about two weeks, especially the rosemary. All herbs can also be kept in ziplock bags in the freezer.

## Fresh ginger

Nothing to do with it but toss it into the vegetable drawer of the fridge and wait to see if it gets moldy. This shouldn't happen for about two weeks.

## Hot dogs

Keep in the fridge or, if you don't eat them that often, in the drawer under the freezer (this will give you about a month, tops). Make sure you check the freshness date on the package.

## Beef

The rule about steak is that the more it costs, the better it is. Buy what you can afford, make sure the date on the package hasn't already passed, then store in the refrigerator if you plan to eat it within three days, or in the freezer if you know only that you'll want it sometime within the next few months. Check and store ground beef, roasts, and stewing meat in the same way. And don't even try to do anything with stewing meat except make stew (p. 126); this is the worst cut of the cow and will be extremely tough unless it is cooked for at least two hours. Keep in mind that the cheaper the ground beef you buy, the more grease you'll find in your pan, and the less meat you'll have once it's cooked. More on beef in chapter 8.

## Poultry

The same rules about checking the dates and storing in the fridge or freezer apply, although we've had friends who have kept a whole chicken in the freezer for three months and are still alive to talk about it. The big concern about poultry, we hope you already know, is salmonella poisoning. It's very important that you rinse off poultry under cold water and pat it dry before you cook it; that you wash off your knife and cutting board and anything else that came into contact with the poultry with water and soap, and that you don't touch anything else (i.e., jars of spices) with your chicken-greased fingers until you've washed them first.

The best poultry deals are usually on whole chickens or packages of thighs or legs (dark meat is always cheaper); cutlets are expensive and so are breasts— especially if the bone's been taken out. If you really have a hankering for a cutlet and want to save some money, buy a breast and pound it down to cutlet thickness by placing it on a cutting board under a piece of Saran Wrap or waxed paper, hammering it with a rolling pin, a thick bottle, or a mallet of some sort. Remember to flip it over and pound from the other side about halfway through this procedure. If you want to bake a chicken (pp. 138-140) but it's only you eating, and you don't want to bother with leftovers or making chicken soup (p. 141), you can splurge on a game hen and cook it in the same way as a big chicken.

*Madhur Jaffrey's Spice Kitchen*, by Madhur Jaffrey

*Italian Cooking for Beginners*, by Helene Siegel

*The Joy of Cooking*, by Irma Rombauer

*The New York Times Cookbook*, by Craig Claiborne

*Jane Brody's Good Food Book*, by Jane Brody

*Jane Brody's Good Food Gourmet*, by Jane Brody

# Bacon

Two things to check before you buy: freshness date, and the little plastic "window" on the back of the package that lets you see how much fat the bacon is packing. Two ways to store once you buy: in the freezer (lasts longer—about three months—but requires that you thaw slightly before cooking), and in the drawer under the freezer, which keeps bacon cool at a temperature slightly below normal fridge level, but above freezing.

## Other meat

Veal, pork, and lamb are all pretty pricey. Check and store in the same way as beef.

## Seafood

If you live in an area where there are fish stores, buy there, but expect to spend a small fortune. Also plan to eat fish the same day you buy it, and keep it in the refrigerator or on ice, even, until the second you cook it. Try not to buy fresh fish at the supermarket; chances are once you see the way it looks smushed up against a cellophane wrapper you'll lose your appetite, anyway. Frozen's the way to go at the supermarket. The best deal: shrimp, which will keep about three months in the freezer.

## Ice cream

Keep it in the freezer. Throw out once it accumulates frost—up to two weeks once it's open.

## Frozen waffles

The same as ice cream. No need to thaw before toasting.

## Cakes and cookies

We like to keep them in the freezer, especially if they contain chocolate in some form. You, however, can keep them anywhere you want. The more preservatives they contain, the longer they'll last. Homemade baked goods usually last about a week in airtight containers before going stale.

## Vanilla extract

Nice to have around, even if you don't do much baking. Keep it in the cabinet; use it in french toast (p. 56).

## Bags of snack food

Potato chips, corn chips, tortilla chips, cheese doodles: Once the bag's open they won't go soggy for about a week if you close the bag back up, especially if you keep them in the fridge.

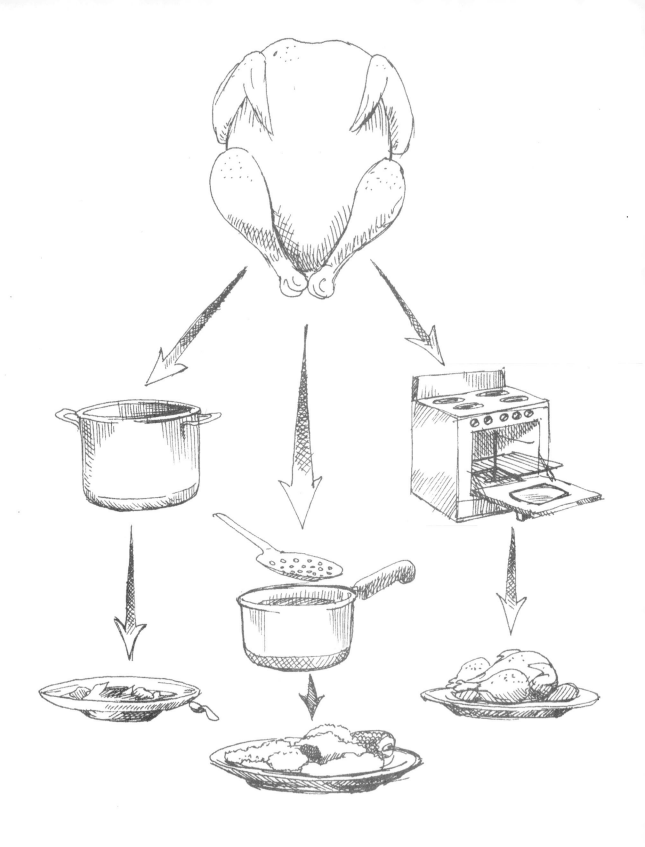

# 3

# *How To Cook What You Bought*

Congratulations. You've got food in your cabinets. You've explored the offerings of aisle three, you've discovered the "Bargain of the Week" section, you've wrestled the last chicken in the store from a senior citizen. But perhaps you still haven't mastered the delicate arts of boiling water and making toast. Following, a primer.

## Food Laws

Did you know that it's against the law: (a) to sell cornflakes on Sunday in Columbus, Ohio, (b) to slurp soup in a public restaurant in New Jersey, (c) to ride any bus or attend any theater in Gary, Indiana, within four hours after eating garlic?

(Source: *Lang's Compendium of Culinary Nonsense and Trivia*, by George Lang)

# How To . . .

## Boil water

Fill a saucepot or stockpot (size to be determined by you) with cold tap water (why cold water remains a mystery, although our guess is that it has something to do with an age-old fear of rusty hot water pipes). Place on the stove over high heat and cover with a lid (this makes it boil faster). Water is boiling when big, foamy bubbles appear on the surface. If you're boiling pasta, potatoes, vegetables, or rice, you'll probably want to add some salt to the water at this stage. Use a palmful for a large stockpot, a level teaspoon or less for a saucepot.

## Make toast

Remove however many slices of pre-sliced bread you think you can eat, or slice up whole leftover bread into one-half to three-quarter inch slices with a serrated knife. There are at least three ways to actually toast the bread.

**In the toaster:** Place slices in the nifty slots on the top of the toaster, set indicator to light, medium, or dark, and push down the lever. The toast will pop up when it's done.

**In the toaster oven:** Set oven to "toast" and place the sliced bread right on the rack. Check it every minute or so until you've achieved desired toastedness.

**In the broiler:** Preheat oven to "broil," that is, set it and allow it to warm up for five minutes. Place the sliced bread in the broiler and close the drawer. Check after two minutes for doneness, then flip onto the other side and toast for another one-two minutes, checking to make sure it isn't burning.

## Grate a carrot

Scrape off the skin with a peeler, then rinse under cold water and cut off the tip of the thin end. With confident, rapid strokes, and a hint of pressure, move the carrot up and down along the fingernail-sized holes of the grater until the whole carrot has vanished and you are left holding the stumpy green end. Like magic, shredded carrot will be revealed when you lift up the grater.

## Chop an onion

With a paring or chef's knife, cut off the root ends of the onion on a cutting board. Make an incision through the onion skin, from one root end to the other, and peel off the skin. Cut the onion in half lengthwise (that is, root end to root end). Lie one half of the onion, flatside down, on the cutting board. Starting at one root end, cut the onion into half-inch slices, then make one horizontal slice in the onion half, parallel to the cutting board.

Cut the onion into small, diced pieces by slicing the onion in the opposite direc-
tion of the first set of
slices. Repeat with
the second
onion half.

## In That Inferno

"Mignon flung open the oven door. Inside, in that inferno, Aida's face grinned the tremendous chortle of the apple-stuffed mouth, her mouth, her forehead wreathed in parsley and laurel and slices of carrot and lemon as for Carnival: tempting for the first fraction of a second, hideous immediately after, the whole world hideous…"

from *A House in the Country*, by Jose Donoso

## Snappy Substitutions

The recipe calls for a clove of garlic but you don't have it and there's no way you're going back out to the supermarket to get it. This does not mean you should order a pizza. Below, a list of substitutions for a few common items:

Garlic: 1 clove = 1 tsp garlic powder

Onion: 1 medium onion = 1 tbsp onion powder

Fresh herbs: 1 tbsp fresh = 1 tsp dried (Note: Do not use dried herbs for garnish—looks stupid, tastes crappy.)

Broth (1 cup): 1 bouillon cube + 1 cup water

Tabasco: 4 dashes = 1 pinch red pepper flakes or cayenne pepper

Lemons/Limes: Use one for the other; or, if you're feeling experimental, substitute an equal amount of orange juice.

## Chop garlic

On a cutting board, crush the clove of garlic under the flat side of the blade of a large knife. Remove the skin, then chop off the root end. Place the smashed garlic clove under the sharp blade of your knife, then move knife handle up and down in a seesawing motion, keeping the tip of the blade on the cutting board. Rearrange the garlic into a pile under your knife and repeat seesawing motion until garlic is chopped to desired fineness.

## Beat eggs

Two eggs are usually sufficient for one person. In one deft motion, crack the first egg on the side of the bowl and empty contents, yolk and all, into said bowl. Remove any bits of shell. Repeat with second egg. With a fork or a medium-sized whisk, beat the eggs with plenty of wrist action and an air of superiority until they are a consistent yellow color. To make scrambled eggs, see p. 52.

## Cook vegetables

**Frozen:** Place unwrapped package of frozen vegetables in medium-sized saucepot, so that they lie flat. Cover bottom of pot with about 1/4 inch of water, place on stove over medium-low flame, and cover. Cook 10-15 minutes, flipping the frozen block of vegetables around as it thaws until vegetables are thoroughly purged of ice. Drain in colander, sprinkle with salt and pepper, and serve.

**Fresh:** To steam, wash vegetables, trim and cut as necessary, and place in a colander. Sprinkle with salt, pepper, and olive oil. Bring a cup of water to a boil in a small stockpot over high flame, place colander on top of pot, and cover. Cook 5-10 minutes, until tender.

To quick-sauté, wash vegetables and trim and cut as necessary. Place in a skillet with enough water to just cover the bottom, sprinkle with salt, pepper, and olive oil, and turn flame on to medium. Cook 5-10 minutes, stirring often, until vegetables are tender. A clove of garlic, smashed in a garlic press, may be added to the skillet with the vegetables.

## Cook Potatoes

**To boil:** Wash potatoes, then peel them or leave the skins on, as you desire. Cut them into 1-inch pieces (unless they're really small), place in a saucepot, and cover with cold water. Place on stove over high flame and bring to a boil. Lower flame to medium and cook for approximately 20 minutes, until tender.

**To bake:** Wash baking potato well, then poke all over with the tines of a fork. Place in a preheated, 350°F oven for about 1 hour, until tender. To get crisp skin, after 1 hour, increase oven temperature to 400°F and bake an additional 15 minutes.

**To fry:** Wash potatoes and slice into thin rounds. Add enough oil to a large, heavy skillet to just cover, and heat over medium flame. Add potatoes with sprinkling of salt and pepper. Cook for approximately 15 minutes, stirring often, until potatoes are nicely browned and crisp all over. Drain on paper towels.

"Something's Burning," by Bob Dylan

"Givin' Up Food for Funk," by the JB's

*1,001 Secrets of Great Cooks*, by Jean Anderson

## Make breadcrumbs

Hack up stale bread (up to 1-1/2 weeks old, if it isn't moldy) with a serrated bread knife or whatever implement seems most likely to render the loaf into two- to three-inch pieces. Place a few bread pieces in blender or food processor, cover with lid, and chop until fine. Empty contents into a plastic storage container and repeat process with remaining bread. Keep breadcrumbs covered in the refrigerator or freezer, indefinitely.

## Reheat leftovers

Leftover chili, stir-fry, and Chinese and Indian take-outs all heat up nicely in the microwave. Stick the whole plate of food right in, set on high for about 5 minutes, and remember to stop cooking time halfway through to stir, so that the food heats evenly. You can also put leftovers in a heavy-bottomed saucepot, add a few tablespoons of water, and heat over a low flame on the stove, stirring often.

Leftover vegetables and Chinese dumplings can be placed in a colander, covered, and reheated over a pot that contains two inches of boiling water, for about five minutes.

Pasta is pretty unappetizing the second day, but not so bad if you heat it up in some broth and consume it like soup. Don't even bother trying to reheat rice — just make it fresh.

Whole pieces of meat can be wrapped in tin foil and placed in a preheated 250°F oven for about 10 minutes, until warmed through. Keep in mind that they'll come out well done.

## Thaw frozen meat and shrimp

Remove frozen meat from the freezer in the morning if you plan to eat it that night. Allow to sit on the counter top for several hours until it's almost completely thawed, then place it in refrigerator until ready to use. Otherwise, about one hour before you want to cook it, place the still-wrapped meat under cold running water until it's thawed.

Remove shrimp from the freezer about one hour before you want to use them and place under cold running water to thaw. As the shrimp begin to thaw, start removing them, one at a time, from the block of ice. Place in a bowl and keep in fridge until ready to use.

### How to Help Someone Who's Choking:

After all these years, the Heimlich Maneuver's still the method of choice.

### How to Choke Someone Who's Helping:

While said someone is engrossed in chopping vegetables in a manner that defies all logic, quietly position yourself behind them, encircle their neck with the fingers of both hands, and squeeze. Release only when they promise to leave the kitchen and never return.

# 4

# *Morning in America: Breakfast*

Maybe the thought of piling on the old pancakes and syrup first thing in the morning makes your precaffeinated stomach seize up. But that's no excuse for not starting the morning off right with a few eye-opening calories. What your mother told you is true: Breakfast is the most important meal of the day. If you have a full day of classes ahead of you, an early nibble will help to ensure that you don't doze off mid-lecture. If you have the misfortune of being required to show up at a job at 9:00 a.m., bright and perky and ready for action, breakfast will allow you to put off lunch until 2:00, maybe even 3:00, which'll make the afternoon fly by.

And don't forget: It isn't really breakfast unless it includes a cup of coffee.

# Coffee

   **10 minutes**

*Even with the proliferation of coffee canteenas sprouting up on every street corner, it's still amazingly difficult to get a decent cup of coffee. If you make it yourself, you can save the $3.00 you would have spent on a mocha latte for a week's worth of bagels.*

**1 tbsp ground coffee**
**1 cup cold water**

1. Place coffee grounds in coffee filter.
2. If using an electric coffee pot, add water, place pot under dribble spout, and turn on. Otherwise, place filter in plastic receptacle over a coffee mug, boil water in a pot, and pour slowly over grounds.
3. Serve in a mug with milk and/or sugar, as desired.

# Espresso

   **10 minutes**

*If the basic cup of American coffee isn't enough to get you going in the morning, drink this.*

**espresso-grind coffee**
**water**

1. Unscrew espresso pot and fill bottom receptacle 3/4 of the way with cold water. Top with metal coffee filter.

2. Spoon espresso into filter, without tamping it down, until filter is full, but not overflowing.

3. Screw on top of espresso pot; place on stove over very low flame. Espresso is ready when you hear a loud whooshing noise emanating from the pot. Remove instantly from flame and serve, with or without milk and sugar.

# Cinnamon Toast

   **10 minutes**

**2 slices bread of your choice**
**butter**
**2 tbsp sugar**
**1 tsp cinnamon**

1. In a bowl, mix sugar and cinnamon together until well combined.

2. Toast the bread in the toaster, toaster oven, or broiler to desired doneness. Remove and place on plate.

3. Butter toast.

4. Pick up one slice of toast and, with a spoon, pour cinnamon–sugar mixture over it. Shake off excess. Repeat with second slice of toast. Eat immediately.

## Hung Over?

Lucky for you we know what to do about it: Cook up some bacon, toast an English Muffin, fry an egg by heating 1/2 tbsp butter or margarine in a small skillet over medium-low flame, cracking egg into it, covering with a lid, and cooking 5-7 minutes, until white is firm and yolk has fogged over. Use spatula to remove egg from skillet; place it on one muffin half, sprinkle with salt and pepper, top with a slice of American cheese, and stick under a preheated broiler for about 1 minute, until the cheese is melted. Top with the other muffin half, and consume immediately. Follow up with Alka Seltzer chaser.

# Scrambled Eggs

   **15 minutes**

**2 eggs**
**1 tbsp water**
**pinch or two of salt**
**black pepper to taste**
**1/2 tbsp butter or margarine**

1. Crack eggs into a bowl, add water, and beat. Add salt and pepper and mix in.

2. In a small skillet, melt the butter over a medium flame. Add eggs and stir constantly with a spoon or fork until well set.

3. Serve on a plate, with toast and bacon if desired, and eat immediately. May also be sprinkled with Tabasco.

 *Mix in 1 small tomato, diced, at the end of step 1.*

 *Mix in 1/4 cup diced or grated cheese of your choice at the end of step 1.*

LOW                    MEDIUM                    HIGH

# Cheese Omelet

   **15 minutes**

**2 eggs**
**1/4 cup cheese of your choice, diced or grated**
  **pinch or two of salt**
**1/4 tsp black pepper**
**1/2 tbsp butter or margarine**

1. In a bowl, whisk together the eggs, salt, and pepper.

2. Melt butter in a small skillet over a medium-low flame. Add eggs. Reduce flame to low and allow to cook until bottom begins to set, about 1 minute.

3. Sprinkle cheese over one half of the omelet.

4. When the eggs are almost completely set (about 3 minutes), lift cheeseless half of the omelet with a spatula and fold over onto the half with cheese. Cover skillet with a plate or lid and cook for an additional 30 seconds.

5. Uncover skillet, move it toward your serving plate and, with the spatula, lift the omelet out onto the plate. Eat right away.

 *Add 1 tbsp chopped parsley in step 1.*

 *Add sliced mushrooms, sautéed for 5 minutes in butter, to cheese side of omelet, in step 3.*

## A Slightly More Questionable Hangover Cure

"Dr. Jarvis's Honey Cure 18 teaspoonsful of honey, to be given 6 at a time, 20 minutes apart. Then repeat in 3 hours. Let patient drink whiskey left by bed if he wishes. Next morning repeat 40-minute honey routine, follow with soft-boiled egg, and then in 10 minutes give 6 more tea-spoonsful honey. For lunch give 4 t. honey, then glass of tomato juice, medium piece of chopped beef, and for dessert 4 more t. honey. Leave whiskey on table toward normal evening meal, but it will probably not be drunk."

from *A Cordiall Water*, by M.F.K. Fisher

*Pancakes & Waffles*, by Elizabeth Alston

*The Good Breakfast Book*, by Nikki & David Goldbeck
(vegetarian)

*The Breakfast Book*, by Marion Cunningham
(complicated)

# Fritata

  　**20 minutes**

**2 eggs**
**1 small potato**
**1/2 small red onion**
**2 tsp oil**
**2 tsp butter or margarine**
**pinch or two of salt**
**black pepper to taste**

1. Wash the potato and slice into thin rounds. Set aside.

2. Peel the onion half and cut into thin rounds. Set aside.

3. Beat the eggs in a bowl with the salt and pepper. Set aside.

4. In a small skillet, heat the oil over a medium flame. Add the potatoes and cook, stirring often, for 5 minutes.

5. Add the onion to the skillet and cook, stirring often, for an additional 5 minutes.

6. Add the butter to the skillet and let it melt. Add the eggs and stir with a fork for about 1 minute. Reduce flame to low.

7. Cover the skillet and allow to cook for an additional 2 minutes. Loosen the fritata around the edges with a spatula, place a plate, serving-side down, over the skillet, and flip upside down. Remove skillet and eat fritata.

　*Top with 1 tbsp chopped parsley.*

# Pancakes

   **30 minutes**

**1 cup white or wheat flour**
**1 heaping tsp baking powder**
**pinch of salt**
**1 cup milk**
**butter or margarine**

1. Preheat oven to 200°F.

2. In a medium bowl, mix all the dry ingredients together with a fork. Add milk and stir to incorporate, but don't worry about getting out all the lumps. If batter is too thick, add more milk, 1 tbsp at a time. If it's too thin, add more flour, 1 tbsp at a time. The batter should be the consistency of thick cream.

3. In a medium skillet over a medium flame, melt 1/2 tbsp butter or margarine. Swirl around until butter glazes the entire surface.

4. When butter is sizzling, spoon 2 tbsp batter onto the skillet to make a 1-1/2 inch pancake. Repeat until no more pancakes fit in the pan.

5. When bubbles appear all over surface of pancakes, flip with a spatula. Cook an additional minute, or until bottom is golden.

6. Place pancakes in an ovenproof dish and put in oven.

7. Repeat steps 3-6 until all the batter is gone. Serve with syrup or alternative toppings.

 *Add 1/4 cup fresh or frozen, thawed berries at the end of step 2.*

## Waffle Toppings that Aren't Syrup

Hands down, we all know waffles are our favorite breakfast food. And why bother making them yourself when you can buy Eggo? Just stick in the toaster and, presto, five minutes later, you've got breakfast. If you're out of maple syrup, try one of these toppings instead:

**Melted Jelly:** Place 2 tbsp jelly in a small saucepot over very low flame. Stir constantly for about 2 minutes, until jelly is completely melted. Remove from flame and pour immediately over two toasted waffles.

**Powdered Sugar:** Put 2 tbsp powdered sugar in a sieve and sprinkle over two toasted waffles.

**Honey & Bananas:** Cut half a banana into thin slices. Arrange in a pattern of your choosing over two toasted waffles and top with honey.

**Butter & Cinnamon Sugar:** Mix 2 tbsp sugar with 1 tsp cinnamon. Spread 1 tbsp butter or margarine over two toasted waffles, then sprinkle with cinnamon sugar.

## The Bagel vs The English Muffin

**Bagel Pros**
1. Comes in at least 15 different flavors.
2. When fresh, it's warm and chewy.
3. Toasted, it's crispy on the outside, soft on the inside.
4. Holds up well under cream cheese.
5. One bagel is usually sufficient for breakfast.

**Bagel Cons**
1. When used for a sandwich, the hole can cause unsightly drippage.
2. Goes stale quick.
3. Jelly is inappropriate for many bagel varieties.

**Muffin Pros**
1. Toasts up nice and crisp.
2. Comes in handy "sandwich" size.
3. The greatest cheese melt base.

**Muffin Cons**
1. No good unless it's toasted.
2. Gets soggy from mayo-based salads.
3. Toasted, those crispy bumps can hurt your gums.

**Final Score**
**Bagel**
    Pros: 5  Cons: 3
**English Muffin**
    Pros: 3  Cons: 3

**The Winner:**
    Bagel by a nose.

# French Toast

    **25 minutes**

**8 slices day old or two-day old bread**
**2 eggs**
**1 cup milk**
**butter or margarine, preferably unsalted**

1. Preheat oven to 200°F.

2. Beat eggs and milk together in a wide, shallow bowl until well combined.

3. Melt 1/2 tbsp butter or margarine in large skillet over medium flame.

4. Dip one slice of bread into egg mixture, making sure to immerse both sides. Allow excess to drip off, then place in skillet. Repeat with second slice of bread.

5. Cook until bottom is brown, 3-5 minutes. Flip with a spatula and cook an additional 2-4 minutes. Remove from skillet, place in ovenproof dish, and put in oven to keep warm.

6. Repeat steps 3-5 with 2 more slices of bread, wipe out skillet with a paper towel, and repeat steps 3-5 with remaining 4 slices of bread.  Serve with syrup or alternate topping of your choice.

*Add 2 tsp cinnamon to egg mixture in step 2.*

*Add 1 tsp vanilla extract to egg mixture in step 2.*

# Bacon

   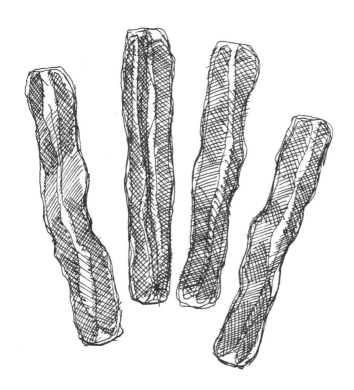 **20 minutes**

**2-4 strips bacon**

1. Heat a medium-sized, heavy-bottomed skillet over a medium flame.

2. Separate strips of bacon. Lay flat on surface of skillet and reduce flame to low. Cook 7-10 minutes, until bottom is crisp. Flip strips over with a fork and cook an additional 3-5 minutes, until crisp all over.

3. Remove bacon from skillet and place on paper towels to drain.

 "I Don't Sleep I Drink Coffee Instead," by Mary's Danish

 "Alan's Psychedelic Breakfast," by Pink Floyd

 "She Don't Use Jelly," by The Flaming Lips

## A Breakfast at Delmonico's, Circa 1893

The estimable Charles Ranhofer, chef of the famous Delmonico's restaurant in New York City of yesteryear, listed eight complete breakfast menus for each month of the year. Here is a random sampling of dishes offered:

Caviare canapés

Sea bass with almond butter

Codfish tongues with chopped sauce

Truffled pig's feet

Guinea fowl with sauerkraut

Broiled bear steak

Turkey wings with turnip

Broiled ptarmigan

Rum omelet

Small green turtles, baked

(Source: *Lang's Compendium of Culinary Nonsense and Trivia*, by George Lang)

# Bisquick Cinnamon Buns

 ||||  20 minutes

**Bisquick**
**1 tbsp sugar**
**unsalted butter**
**brown sugar**
**cinnamon**

1. Follow directions on the Bisquick box for biscuits, but add 1 tbsp sugar to the mix.
2. Mix well with your hand or a spoon.
3. Sprinkle a handful of Bisquick onto a cutting board, and roll out the biscuit dough to about 1/4 of an inch thick with a rolling pin or a heavy bottle.
4. Dot the surface of the rolled out dough with bits of unsalted butter; sprinkle liberally with brown sugar and cinnamon.
5. Roll up the dough to make a log. Cut the log into 1-inch discs and place flat, nestled closely together, in a buttered baking dish or on a buttered baking sheet.
6. Sprinkle tops of biscuits with more brown sugar and cinnamon, and top with more bits of unsalted butter.
7. Place in preheated 450°F oven and bake about 10 minutes, until slightly brown around the edges.

 *Add 2 tbsp chopped walnuts or raisins in step 4.*

# 5
# *Surf and Turf: Soups and Sandwiches*

## Soup: The Liquid Lunch

There's just no arguing with a good bowl of soup. Ingested when it's at the ideal temperature—a few degrees above your body's—it'll make you feel warm and fuzzy all over, like everything is right with the world. If you scoff at the idea of eating only soup for a meal, increase your calorie intake by pairing it with a sandwich, or make it a starter course at dinner.

## Fine Homemade Mushroom Soup

"Take one package Knorr Mushroom Soup mix. Prepare as directed. Take four large mushrooms. Slice. Throw into Soupmix. Throw in 1/2 cup Tribuno Dry Vermouth, parsley, salt, pepper. Stick bread... into soup at intervals. Buttering bread enhances taste of the whole."

Knorr is a very good Swiss outfit whose products can be found in both major and minor cities. The point here is not to be afraid of the potential soup but to approach it with the attitude that you know what's best for it. And you do.

from *The Teachings of Don B.*, by Donald Barthelme

# Egg Drop Soup

    **10 minutes**

**15-oz can chicken broth, or
  2 chicken bouillon cubes + 2 cups cold
  water**
**1 egg**
**black pepper to taste**

1. In a medium saucepan, heat the chicken broth, or bouillon cubes and water, over a low flame.
2. While the broth is heating, beat the egg in a medium bowl with a fork until well combined.
3. When the broth is boiling (if using bouillon cubes, make sure they've dissolved thoroughly), add the eggs in a slow, steady stream, mixing the broth constantly with a fork.
4. Remove broth from heat and add pepper to taste.
5. Divide soup evenly between two bowls. Serve with large spoons, if possible.

 *Top each bowl of soup with 1 tbsp chopped scallions, green part only.*

 *Add 1/4 cup frozen peas at beginning of step 1.*

# Vichyssoise

    **45 minutes**

LEEK

**2 large potatoes**
**1 leek, white part only**
**2 tbsp butter or margarine**
**3/4 cup milk**
**1-3/4 cups chicken broth**
**salt**
**black pepper**

1. Wash and peel the potatoes and cut into 2-inch pieces. Place in a medium saucepot and cover with water. Bring to a boil over high heat, reduce flame to medium-low and cook approximately 20 minutes, until tender.

2. While the potatoes are cooking, wash the white part of the leek and chop it. Melt the butter in a skillet over a low flame, add the leek, a pinch of salt, a pinch of black pepper, and cook 5-7 minutes, stirring often, until soft.

3. When the potatoes are cooked, drain them and rinse under cold water until cool to the touch. Place half of them in a blender. Add half the leek mixture and half the chicken broth. Cover with lid and blend until smooth. Pour into a pot.

4. Repeat step 3 with remaining potatoes, leek, and chicken broth. Add to pot. Turn on flame to low and add milk, stirring constantly until soup is warmed through (do not let it boil).

5. Serve immediately or let sit in the refrigerator, covered, for 1 hour, and serve cold.

 *Add 2 tbsp fresh chopped dill at the end of step 4.*

## Mushroom Soup Rules

According to *Newsweek* (September 25, 1995), more than a million cans of Campbell's cream-of-mushroom soup "are used in dinner recipes every day." Which compels us to ask the eternal, nagging question: "Why?"

# Carrot and Cauliflower Soup

   **20 minutes**

**1 small head cauliflower**
**2 carrots**
**1/2 tsp salt**
**1-1/2 cups chicken broth**
**1/2 cup milk**
**1/4 tsp black pepper**

1. Wash cauliflower. Cut off and discard stem and cut head into florets.

2. Peel and slice carrots. Place vegetables in large pot with 1/2 tsp salt and cover with cold water. Bring to a boil over high flame, reduce flame to medium-low and cook until tender, about 10 minutes.

3. Drain vegetables into a colander and place half in a blender. Add half the chicken broth, cover with lid, and puree until smooth. Empty into large bowl.

4. Repeat step 3 with the remaining vegetables and chicken broth. Add to the first batch of soup.

5. Add milk to the soup and stir to incorporate. Taste for seasoning and add pepper as desired. Divide evenly between two bowls and eat.

# Oriental Chicken Soup

   5 minutes

**1 cup chicken broth**
**juice of 1/2 lime**
**1/4 tsp black pepper**
**1 tbsp chopped fresh cilantro, leaves only**

1. Heat chicken broth in small saucepot over low flame. Place in bowl.

2. Add lime juice, pepper, and cilantro, and stir. Eat while it's hot.

 *Add red pepper flakes in step 2.*

# Leftover Lentil Soup

   5 minutes

**1/4 cup cooked, leftover lentils**
**1 cup chicken broth**

1. Place lentils and chicken broth in a small saucepot and heat over low flame, about 5 minutes.

2. Remove from heat and eat.

 *Before heating lentils and broth, peel and dice a carrot, cover with water, and boil until tender, about 10 minutes. Drain and add to soup at end of step 1.*

# Cream of Tomato Soup

     **30 minutes**

**2 lbs very ripe tomatoes**
**1 small onion**
**2 tbsp oil**
**2 tbsp butter or margarine**
**1/4 cup chicken broth**
**6-oz heavy cream**
**2 tsp salt**
**2 tsp black pepper**
**1 tsp sugar**

1. Wash and dice tomatoes. Set aside.

2. Chop onion and set aside.

3. Heat oil and butter or margarine in a medium skillet over medium flame and add onion. Cook, stirring constantly, for about 5 minutes, until translucent. Add tomatoes, salt, pepper, and sugar, increase flame to high, and cook 5-7 minutes, until tomatoes have oozed most of their liquid. Don't forget to stir often.

4. Put tomato mixture in a blender. Add chicken broth and puree until smooth. Transfer to a bowl and stir in cream. Serve immediately.

*Add 2 tbsp fresh chopped dill (no stems) at end of step 4.*

# Sandwiches: The Solid Lunch

You can shove almost anything between two slices of bread (or into a pita, a roll, a bagel, or an English muffin) and call it a sandwich. Food combinations never found in nature seem somehow appealing when hunger strikes and the larder yields only a loaf of Wonder, a hunk of leftover meatloaf, and some jelly. A favorite sandwich of a childhood friend of ours was peanut butter, mayo, and pickles. Hopefully, you will never be desperate enough to resort to eating such "interesting" creations, but if they sound good to you, who are we to argue? Following, a number of more traditional sandwich suggestions.

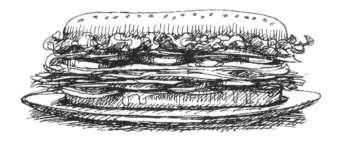

## The Masterpiece

John Montagu, the fourth Earl of Sandwich, invented the masterpiece that bears his name during a 24-hour stint at the gambling table in 1762. Reluctant to break for a proper meal, he ordered a piece of beef and held it between two slices of bread so he could continue his winning streak uninterrupted.

## Peanut Butter and You

Unless you've been waited on by servants all your life, you probably know how to spread peanut butter on bread to make a sandwich. You may even know how to add jelly. Here are some other excellent peanut butter ideas you may not have thought of.

With banana: Add half a sliced banana to the classic peanut butter sandwich.

With cinnamon: Sprinkle the inside of the sandwich with cinnamon.

On apples: With a small, sharp knife, cut apple (preferably a Granny Smith) into quarters, remove core, peel if you want, and slather each quarter with peanut butter.

On celery: Wash however many celery stalks you think you can reasonably consume in one sitting. Trim off thick end, cut into 3-inch pieces, and fill cavities with peanut butter.

On corn chips: One at a time, dip corn chips into peanut butter. Place in mouth. Chew and swallow.

# Grilled Cheese

   **15 minutes**

**2 slices bread**
**2 slices American or other sliced cheese**
**1 tbsp butter or margarine**

1.  Layer the cheese on one slice of bread. Top with the other slice of bread.

2.  In a skillet, melt half the butter over medium heat and swirl pan to glaze evenly. Add sandwich, reduce flame to low, cover skillet with a lid, and let cook until brown on the bottom, 3-5 minutes.

3.  Lift out sandwich with a spatula, add remaining butter to the pan and swirl to cover. Flip sandwich over onto skillet and re-cover. Cook an additional 2-4 minutes, until second side is brown and cheese is melted. Remove from skillet with spatula and serve.

*Cut a small tomato into thin rounds and place on top of cheese in step 1. Follow directions through step 3.*

*In a small skillet, fry 2 pieces of bacon and drain on paper towels. Place on top of cheese in step 1. Follow directions through step 3.*

*Crocque Monsieur, the French answer to junk food: Coat one side each slice of bread with mayonnaise. Top with cheese and 1 slice of ham. Follow directions through step 3.*

# Spinach and Cheese Pita Melt

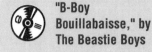

"B-Boy Bouillabaisse," by The Beastie Boys

   **15 minutes**

*Since the spinach, when you take it out of the freezer, will be a solid block of green ice and therefore tricky to split in half unless you have a chain saw at your disposal, your best bet is to cook up the whole package and store half of it in a plastic container in the refrigerator for later use (to reheat, see p. 46).*

**1/2 package frozen spinach**
**2 slices American or other sliced cheese**
**1 pita**

1.  Preheat oven or toaster oven to 350°F.

2.  Cook the spinach, drain it in a colander, then squeeze it dry with your hands. Put half away in the refrigerator, set the other half aside.

3.  While the spinach is cooking, put the pita in the oven until it puffs up, 2-4 minutes. Remove and make a large slit around one edge.

4.  Fill pita with spinach and cheese, place it on a piece of tin foil, and place back in oven for 5 minutes, or until cheese is completely melted. Eat up.

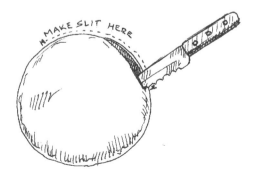

## Seeds Stop Smoking

Everyone we know has quit smoking five times in the last year. Some have tried the patch, others, nicotine gum; one determined soul handcuffed himself to his bed for two weeks (now that we think about it, we're not sure he was ever a smoker). The results were mixed, but the clear winner was Bronwyn Orosco, who quit smoking by eating handfuls of sunflower seeds every time she was in need of an oral fixation. Says Bronwyn: "They really worked. Apparently, it's not just keeping your mouth busy, there's a chemical reaction that helps reduce the urge or does the same thing as nicotine."

# Baked Beans on Toast

   **10 minutes**

*This is only a pseudo-sandwich; a knife and fork are nearly imperative for consumption.*

### 10-oz can baked beans
### 2 slices bread

1.  Open the can of beans and empty contents into a small saucepot. Place on stove over low heat, and stir occasionally so beans get heated evenly through, 5-7 minutes.

2.  While the beans are warming, toast the bread. Place on a plate and top with the warmed baked beans.

# Tuna: A Lifesaver

There's almost no way you can ruin a can of tuna. Not only is it tasty and good for you, its shelf life (in the unopened can) is longer than yours. And always get tuna-in-water. It has fewer calories than tuna-in-oil, and it tastes better too.

# The Classic Tuna Sandwich

   **5 minutes**

**1 can tuna**
**1 tbsp mayonnaise, or more, if desired**
**salt and black pepper to taste**
**4 slices bread**

1. Open tuna with a can opener. Drain and place in a bowl.
2. Add mayo, salt, and pepper and mix with a fork. Spread on 2 slices of bread and cover with remaining 2 slices of bread.

 *Add half a small chopped onion.*

 *Add two chopped celery stalks.*

## Eating Out

Sure, everyone likes to eat out once in a while; and maybe, if you're lucky, one day you'll be able to afford it, too. When that day finally arrives, you probably won't want to spend every single penny in your bank account. Start out slow, start out frugal, with a restaurant not completely beyond your budget. To do this, you'll need to have a peek at the menu first; some catch phrases to look for that will indicate this restaurant is way out of your league, even before you see the prices:

1. Au jus
2. Tartare
3. Melange
4. Service compris
5. Chateau Mouton de

# Tuna with Oil and Garlic

   10 minutes

**1 can tuna**
**1 tbsp olive oil**
**1 small clove garlic**
**salt and black pepper to taste**
**4 slices bread**

1. Open tuna, drain, and place in bowl.
2. Add oil, salt, and pepper.
3. Remove skin from garlic, place clove in garlic press, and squeeze into tuna (or, chop garlic as fine as you can with a sharp knife).
4. Mix well and serve between bread slices.

# Tuna with Italian Dressing

   10 minutes

**1 can tuna**
**1 tbsp Italian dressing, jarred or homemade (p. 84)**
**4 slices bread**

1. Open tuna, drain, and place in bowl.
2. Mix dressing well and add to tuna. Combine with a fork and place on bread.

# Tuna with Tomato and Basil

   10 minutes

**1 can tuna**
**1 small tomato**
**1 sprig basil, leaves only**
**2 tbsp olive oil**
**salt and black pepper to taste**
**4 slices bread**

1.  Open tuna, drain, and place in bowl.

2.  Wash tomato, remove core, and dice. Add to tuna.

3.  Wash basil leaves, dry on paper towels, chop, and add
    to tuna with oil, salt, and pepper. Mix well with a fork.

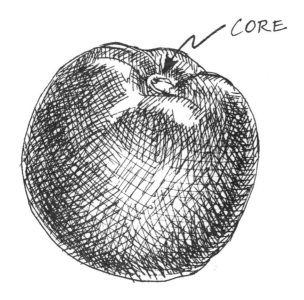

CORE

# Tuna with Beans

   10 minutes

1 can tuna
1/4 cup white kidney beans, rinsed and
    drained
1/2 tbsp vinegar, preferably balsamic
1-1/2 tbsp olive oil
salt and black pepper to taste
4 slices bread

1. Open tuna, drain, and place in bowl.
2. Add remaining ingredients, minus bread, to tuna and mix
   well. Make into sandwiches.

# Tuna with Sunflower Seeds

   5 minutes

1 can tuna
1 tbsp mayonnaise, or more if desired
2 tbsp sunflower seeds
pinch or two salt
1/4 tsp black pepper
4 slices bread

1. Open tuna, drain, and place in bowl.
2. Add all remaining ingredients except bread and mix
   well. Serve on bread.

# Tuna Melt

   15 minutes

**1 can tuna**
**1 tsp oil**
**pinch or two salt**
**1/4 tsp black pepper**
**2 slices American or other sliced cheese**
**1 bagel, or 2 slices bread**

1. Preheat oven or toaster oven to broil.

2. Open tuna, drain, and place in bowl.

3. Add oil, salt, and pepper to tuna and mix well to combine.

4. Cut bagel in half. Place bagel or bread slices in broiler, and toast. Remove.

5. Place bagel slices or toast on piece of tin foil. Divide tuna mixture evenly between them and top with cheese. Place back in broiler and cook until cheese is melted and bubbly, about 2 minutes. Remove and eat.

## The Sandwich vs The Hero

It's easy to tell the difference, really. A sandwich is a delicate item, consisting of a slice or two of luncheon meat neatly inserted between bread slices, decorated with a pretty frill of lettuce or tomato, and saved from absolute blandness by a wipe of mustard or mayo. Now a hero, that's a different story. Ideally, a hero should be no shorter than your dining table, no longer than your kitchen. It should contain at least three varieties of meat. Add sliced tomatoes, lettuce, onions, peppers, olives, mustard, mayo, salad dressing, and, oh yeah, a pound or so of cheese; put it all together (you win no points here for "technique" that's for sandwich eaters), slice up on an angle, and get busy.

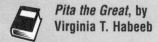 *Pita the Great*, by Virginia T. Habeeb

# Egg Salad

   **40 minutes**

**4 eggs**
**1 tbsp mayonnaise**
**1 tsp mustard**
**1/2 tsp salt**
**1/4 tsp black pepper**
**4 slices bread**

1. Take the eggs out of the refrigerator and let them sit at room temperature for about 10 minutes (this way, they won't crack when you boil them).

2. Fill a medium saucepot about 3/4 of the way with water and bring to a boil over high flame. Add eggs to the water, one at a time, by putting them on a large spoon and carefully dropping them into the water. Reduce flame to low. Cook eggs 20 minutes, then remove pot from stove and place under cold running water. Let the eggs sit in cold water about 5 minutes, until shells are cool to the touch.

3. With the back of a teaspoon, crack the eggshells, remove and discard them. Cut the eggs into 2-inch pieces and place them in a medium-sized bowl.

4. Add the mayo, mustard, salt, and pepper and smash together with the back of a fork until ingredients are well-combined and eggs are the consistency you like. Make into sandwiches.

 *Add 1 tsp horseradish in step 4.*

# Progresso Chicken Vegetable Soup

*Progresso is our favorite canned soup, well worth the extra 30 or 40 cents it costs over Campbells. No, Progresso is not paying us to recommend them (though we wish they would).*

     **20 minutes**

**1 can Progresso chicken soup**
**1/4 lb of pasta**
**3 cloves garlic**
**3 tbsp water**
**4 dashes Tabasco sauce**

1.  Cook about 1/4 lb of the pasta of your choice, but don't add salt to the water.

2.  Drain into a colander and set aside. Put the soup into the empty pasta pot with 4 dashes of Tabasco, 3 cloves of finely chopped garlic, and 3 tbsp water. Heat through.

3.  Add drained pasta, and serve.

# 6

# *Greens are Good: Salads*

A salad does not necessarily have to be a plate of frilly greens, although we readily admit to eating—and enjoying—many such salads. Even if you are a professed salad-hater, you may find among these recipes an easy, tasty way to get the roughage your system so desperately needs. Here are some suggestions for salads, both frilly and otherwise.

## How to Dye Clothes with Beets

Wash 10 pounds of beets, place in an enamel container, cover with three-and-a-half gallons of water and cook until soft. Add garment that has been treated with alum mordant to the beet bath and simmer for thirty minutes. Add four tablespoons tartaric acid and half a cup of Glauber's salts dissolved in one pint hot water to dye bath; simmer another thirty minutes. Cool, then rinse yarn in warm water until water runs clear. Hang in the shade to dry. Note: Beets may be removed from water after cooking and used as food.

(Source: *Vegetable Dyeing*, by Alma Lesch)

# Beet Salad

    1 hour and 15 minutes

**15-oz can beets**
**1/4 cup Italian dressing, jarred or homemade (p. 84)**

1.  Open beets with a can opener. Drain into a colander and place in medium-sized bowl.

2.  Add dressing; mix well.

3.  Cover bowl with a plate or Saran Wrap and refrigerate for at least 1 hour before serving.

 *Add 2 tbsp chopped fresh dill (no stems) in step 2.*

 *Add 1 small red onion, sliced into thin rounds, in step 1, and increase salad dressing to 1/3 cup.*

# Three Bean Salad

   20 minutes

**10-oz can chickpeas**
**15-oz can red kidney beans**
**1 package frozen green beans or 1 cup fresh**
**1/2 cup Italian dressing with mustard (p. 84)**

1. Cook the green beans in a medium-sized saucepot. Drain and pat dry with paper towels. Place in a large bowl.

2. Open the chickpeas and kidney beans. Pour into a colander and rinse under cold water. Drain, pat dry with paper towels, add to green beans.

3. Add salad dressing to beans and  mix well. Cover bowl with a plate or Saran wrap and refrigerate for at least 1 hour before serving.

 *Add 2 tbsp fresh chopped dill at the beginning of step 3.*

**Cole Slaw . . .**

is the anglicized version of
the Dutch term  koolsla,
meaning "cold" (kool)
"salad" (sla).

# Cole Slaw

   **40 minutes**

**1 small green cabbage**
**1/2 cup Italian dressing**
**1/4 cup mayonnaise**

1. With a large, sharp knife, chop the cabbage by halving
   it lengthwise, cutting out the stem, then slicing into thin
   strips. Place in a large bowl.

2. In a medium-sized bowl, mix the dressing with the mayonnaise and stir with a fork until smooth.

3. Add dressing mixture to cabbage; mix well to combine
   (use your hands). Cover bowl with a plate or Saran
   Wrap and let sit at room temperature for 1/2 an hour
   before serving.

# Fiesta Cole Slaw

   20 minutes

**1 small purple cabbage**

**2 carrots**

**1/2 cup Italian dressing, mustard variation (p. 84)**

**1/4 cup mayonnaise**

1. Cut cabbage as instructed in step 1 of Cole Slaw recipe on previous page. Place in a large bowl.

2. Peel and grate the carrots and add to the cabbage.

3. Follow steps 2-3 of Cole Slaw recipe.

 *Add 1 tbsp celery seeds in step 2.*

## You Wanna Make Your Own Salad Dressing?

We're so proud. Below, several variations:

**Basic Italian Dressing**
Yields 1/2 cup dressing, or 8 servings

    1/2 cup +1 tsp olive oil

    2 1/2 tbsp red wine or balsamic vinegar

    1 tsp salt

    1/2 tsp black pepper

Place all the ingredients in a small bowl and whisk together. Store at room temperature in a jar with a lid.

**With mustard:** Add 1-1/2 tbsp mustard, preferably Dijon.

**Creamy:** Add 1 tbsp mayonnaise.

**With fresh herbs:** Add 2 tbsp chopped fresh dill, marjoram, thyme, etc.

**Oriental:** Substitute juice of 1 lemon for vinegar, replace salt with 1-1/2 tsp soy sauce, and add pinch sugar, 1/2 tsp dry mustard or wasabi, and 1 tsp grated fresh ginger.

# Caesar Salad

    **10 minutes**

**10 large Romaine lettuce leaves**
**2 tbsp mayonnaise**
**4 tbsp oil, preferably olive**
**1 tsp fresh lemon juice**
**1-1/2 tbsp grated Parmesan cheese**
**1/4 tsp salt**
**1/4 tsp black pepper**
**1 large clove finely chopped garlic**
**1/2 cup croutons**

1. Wash and dry lettuce leaves. Rip them into 2-inch pieces and place in medium-sized bowl.

2. In a small bowl, mix mayonnaise, oil, lemon juice, cheese, garlic, salt, and pepper with a fork until well incorporated. Pour over lettuce and mix well.

3. Divide salad evenly between 2 plates. Top with croutons and additional Parmesan and pepper, if desired.

*Add 1 tsp anchovy paste to mayonnaise in step 2, or top each mixed salad with 4 whole anchovies.*

# Mixed Green Salad

   **5-10 minutes**

**10 large or 20 small lettuce leaves of your choice (i.e., bib, Boston, red leaf, green leaf, chicory, or a combination)**
**1/4 cup Italian dressing (p. 84 for homemade)**

1. Wash and dry lettuce. Place in medium-sized bowl.
2. Top with dressing and mix well. Divide evenly between two plates or bowls.

*Add chopped tomatoes, carrots, red onion, red/green peppers, and/or cucumbers in step 1.*

# Potato Salad #1

   **1-1/2 hours**

**1 lb potatoes**
**3 tbsp mayonnaise**
**1 tbsp oil**
**1/2 tbsp vinegar**
**1 tsp + 1/4 tsp salt**
**1/4 tsp black pepper**

1. Wash the potatoes well, cut them into 2-inch pieces, and place in a large saucepot or small stockpot. Cover with cold water, add 1 tsp salt, and bring to a boil over high heat. Lower flame to medium-low and cook potatoes until tender, about 20 minutes.

2. Drain potatoes in a colander and run under cold water until cool to the touch. Pat dry with paper towels and transfer to a medium-sized bowl. Add remaining ingredients and mix well. Cover with a plate or Saran Wrap and refrigerate for at least 1 hour before serving.

# Potato Salad #2

   **30 minutes**

**1 lb potatoes**
**1-1/2 tbsp mayonnaise**
**1/2 tbsp mustard, preferably wholegrain**
**1 tbsp oil**
**1 tsp red wine vinegar**
**salt and pepper to taste**
**pinch sugar**

1. Follow step 1 for Potato Salad #1.
2. Mix remaining ingredients in medium-sized bowl. Add cooked, drained potatoes, and mix well to combine. Serve warm.

 *Fry 2 strips bacon, drain, and crumble. Add in step 2.*

# Tabouli

   **2 hours**

1 cup bulgar wheat
6 cups boiling water
1 clove minced garlic
jarred or homemade salad dressing

**Any or all of the following:**
2 small tomatoes, diced
1/2 cucumber, diced
5 sprigs fresh parsley, leaves only, chopped

1. Rinse the bulgar, place in a large bowl, and cover with boiling water. Cover and allow to sit 15-20 minutes, until bulgar is tender.

2. Drain the bulgar. Place back in bowl and add vegetables, if desired. Add garlic and salad dressing to taste; cover and place in refrigerator for 1 hour before serving.

# Clean Out the Fridge Salad

   **5-15 minutes**

Well, what have you got in there? Boiled potatoes? Some leftover broccoli? The still crisp heart of an otherwise molding head of lettuce? Chop or break it all up into bite-sized pieces, add a can of rinsed and drained beans, some diced celery or carrots, the meat off that chicken wing you've been saving for God knows what, throw it into a bowl, and mix it up with some Italian dressing. It may not look pretty, but we swear, it's a meal.

## Anchovies: Fishy, Salty Nirvana

Slowly but surely, over the years, we have been getting rid of some of our friends, and it all has to do with anchovies: We love them, they hate them. And while to you this may seem a superficial reason for abandoning years-long acquaintanceships, to us, the whole anchovy-hating situation was getting way out of hand: When we wanted to order pizza, they wouldn't let us order anchovies; when we wanted to make Caesar salad, they wouldn't let us add anchovies; when we whipped up a fancy French olive spread whose recipe demanded the inclusion of anchovies, they refused to eat it. Something had to be done. The result: Our kitchen cabinet now contains not one, not three, but seven jars of imported anchovies. Our social calendar's looking a bit sickly, but hey, it's quality, not quantity.

# 7

# *Noodles: Our Favorite Blank Slate*

Ah, noodles, the most delectable of all carbohydrates. Personally, we haven't called noodles "noodles" since we were knee-high to a June bug, whatever that means, but "pasta" isn't quite as all-encompassing a word as your average yuppie would have you believe. Think of pasta as any kind of noodle product that has an Italian-sounding name. Everything else is just noodles.

# One Box of Spaghetti, Twenty Ways to Cover It

Or maybe you have ten boxes of spaghetti, wisely purchased by you when they were on special at the supermarket for 15 cents a pound, and now you're cringing at the thought of having to eat it all. Never fear: following are twenty ways you can sauce up a plate of spaghetti without getting sick of it.

And don't be afraid to experiment with other types of pasta: linguini, fettuccine, cappelini, and percciateli are great substitutes for spaghetti when you're still in the mood for a long noodle; ziti, oreccieti, tagliatelle, penne, farfalle, and rigatoni all have different enough textures to confuse your palate into believing you're eating a substance completely different from spaghetti. We prefer the smaller shapes of pasta (pastina, orzo, tiny shells, ditalini) in broth or covered with just butter and cheese.

## How to Cook Enough Spaghetti for Two People

1. In a large stockpot, bring 8 quarts of cold water to a boil over high heat.

2. When the water is boiling, add a palmful of salt and half a pound of spaghetti, and stir immediately with a large fork to ensure that all the strands are separated. Stir several more times during cooking (always check the package instructions, and try a piece every once in a while to make sure it isn't over or undercooked).

3. When the spaghetti is cooked to the desired state of mushiness, drain into a colander. Then, top with one of the following sauces.

# Lemon and Garlic Spaghetti

    **5minutes**

**4 tbsp olive oil**
**juice of 1/2 lemon**
**4 cloves garlic**
**salt and black pepper to taste**
**grated Parmesan cheese**

1. While the spaghetti water is boiling: Cut the lemon in half widthwise; crush the cloves of garlic with the flat side of a large knife, then remove the skin and chop coarsely.

2. Three minutes before the spaghetti is cooked, heat the oil in a small skillet over a medium flame. Add garlic, salt, and pepper, stirring constantly until garlic begins to brown slightly around the edges, about 1-1/2 minutes. Turn off flame and squeeze the lemon juice into the oil, using a fork to remove any seeds that fall into the mixture.

3. Add the oil-lemon-garlic mixture to the drained spaghetti and mix well. Divide evenly between two plates and top with Parmesan cheese.

*Top each plate of spaghetti with 1 tbsp chopped fresh parsley.*

## Spaghetti Spoons

Every once in a while, you catch sight of one of those curious people who transfer spaghetti from fork to mouth by twirling it on a large spoon. It always looks impressive, but frankly, we've never been able to master the technique. We prefer to shovel the spaghetti straight into our mouth; it dangles against our chin for several moments as we chew, bovine like, before we discard of the excess by cutting off the external strands with our tongue and teeth. It's a little sloppy, but we like to have our second hand free to hold on to the bottle of Chianti.

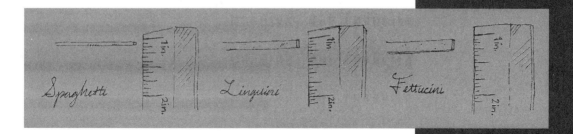

# Carrots and Cheese Spaghetti

   15 minutes

**2 carrots, peeled and cut into rounds**
**1/4 cup butter**
**salt to taste**
**1/4 cup grated Parmesan cheese**

1. While the spaghetti water is boiling, bring a medium-sized pot of water to boil; add cut carrots and cook until tender, about 10 minutes. Drain and set aside.

2. Add butter, carrots, salt, and cheese to cooked and drained spaghetti. Mix well and divide evenly between two plates.

# Broccoli and Garlic Spaghetti

   20 minutes

**1 small head broccoli**
**2 cloves garlic**
**1/3 + 1/4 cup olive oil**
**1/4 cup water**
**salt and black pepper to taste**
**4 tbsp grated Parmesan cheese**

1. While the spaghetti water is boiling: Cut broccoli into florets (that is, cut away the stem so that broccoli falls away into bite-sized pieces); chop garlic; and place 1/4 cup of the oil, the water, broccoli, garlic, salt, and pepper in a large skillet over medium-high flame.

2. Stir broccoli mixture often so that the garlic doesn't stick or burn, for 5-7 minutes, until broccoli has turned a vivid green not usually witnessed in nature. Remove from the flame.

3. Add broccoli mixture to cooked spaghetti along with remaining oil and Parmesan. Mix well and serve.

# Easy Tomato Sauce

    **5 minutes**

**1/2 cup Pomi strained tomatoes**
**1/4 tsp salt**
**pinch black pepper**
**pinch sugar**
**1 tsp olive oil**
**4 tbsp grated Parmesan (optional)**

1. Five minutes before spaghetti is cooked, place tomatoes, salt, pepper, oil, and sugar in a medium saucepot, mix well, and heat over low flame, stirring occasionally. Allow to cook about 5 minutes, until bubbly. Remove from flame and serve over cooked spaghetti. Top with Parmesan.

*Top each plate of spaghetti with 1 tbsp chopped fresh basil.*

## How to Portion Tomato Paste

If a recipe calls for only a tablespoon or so of tomato paste, one if faced with a difficult problem: how to store the remains of the tomato paste without their turning brown. The solution is to open both ends of the can when you buy it. Remove the lid from one end and use the other lid to push the tomato paste through the can and out the open end, onto a piece of plastic wrap. Wrap it up and place it in the freezer. Once the tomato paste log is frozen, you can remove and slice off as much as you need, returning the unused portion to the freezer for as long as it lasts.

# Fresh Tomato Sauce

   **15 minutes**

**2 lbs ripe tomatoes**
**2 cloves garlic**
**5 sprigs flat Italian parsley, leaves only**
**2 tbsp olive oil**
**1/2 tsp sugar**
**1/2 tsp salt**
**1/4 tsp black pepper**
**4 tbsp grated Parmesan cheese**

1. While the spaghetti water is boiling: Chop the tomatoes and garlic; wash parsley, and remove leaves from stems.

2. Ten minutes before spaghetti is cooked, heat the oil in medium-sized skillet over medium-high heat. Add tomatoes, garlic, parsley, sugar, salt, and pepper; stir constantly for about 5 minutes, until tomatoes start giving off liquid.

3. Remove from heat, and serve over cooked spaghetti. Top with grated Parmesan.

# Fancy Tomato Sauce

   **35 minutes**

*Since you're going to all the trouble of making a fancy tomato sauce, invite a few friends over. See if you can get them to bring the wine. Remember to double the amount of spaghetti you make to 1 pound.*

**3 tbsp olive oil**
**4 cloves garlic**
**28-oz can whole Italian tomatoes**
**1/4 cup dry wine, preferably red**
**10 sprigs fresh parsley**
**5 sprigs fresh basil**
**salt and black pepper to taste**
**few pinches sugar**
**grated Parmesan cheese**

1. Before you put the spaghetti water on to boil, open the can of tomatoes and drain off the liquid. Set aside.

2. Chop the garlic and set aside.

3. Wash the parsley and basil, remove leaves from stems, and chop. Set aside.

4. While spaghetti water is boiling, heat the oil in a large skillet over a medium flame. Add garlic and cook for 1 minute, stirring constantly so it doesn't brown or burn. Add the tomatoes, chopping them up with a spoon; then add the wine, parsley, basil, salt, pepper, and sugar, and stir. Reduce flame to medium-low and stir every 5 minutes. Check for seasoning and add more salt, pepper, or sugar as necessary.

5. By the time the spaghetti is almost cooked, the sauce should have lost most of its liquid and look and smell relatively appetizing. If it gets to this stage before the pasta is done, just remove it from the heat and keep it covered until you're ready to use it. If it's too liquidy and the spaghetti is almost ready to be drained, just turn up the heat a bit to quicken the thickening process.

6. Place pasta in a large bowl and top with sauce. Place on table with serving spoon and fork, give your guests some plates, and let them serve themselves and sprinkle on their own Parmesan cheese.

# Meat Sauce

   **60 minutes**

**1 lb ground beef**
**4 cloves crushed garlic**
**28-oz can crushed tomatoes**
**3 tbsp olive oil**
**sugar, salt, and black pepper to taste**
**1/2 cup dry red or white wine**
**grated Parmesan cheese**

1. Heat oil in a large skillet over medium flame; add the garlic and cook about 1 minute, stirring constantly so that it doesn't brown or burn. Put spaghetti water on to boil.

2. Add ground beef to skillet and cook 2-3 minutes, until it's browned all over, stirring occasionally to break up the pieces. Drain off fat into the sink.

3. Add the tomatoes, sugar, salt, pepper, and wine if desired; mix well. Stir occasionally, and taste for seasoning (add more salt and pepper if you want). Desired consistency is about the same as for Fancy Tomato Sauce. Serve over cooked spaghetti, with Parmesan.

*Add any of the other ingredients called for in Fancy Tomato Sauce.*

# Onion and Parsley Sauce

   **10 minutes**

1/4 cup olive oil
1 large yellow onion, sliced into thin rounds
1/4 cup flat Italian parsley, leaves only,
   washed, patted dry, and coarsely chopped
3/4 tsp salt
1/4 tsp black pepper
juice of 1 lemon
grated Parmesan cheese

1. Ten minutes before spaghetti is done, heat oil in a small skillet over medium flame and add the onion, salt, and pepper. Cook 2-3 minutes, until onion is translucent, stirring often.

2 Add parsley and stir to combine. Remove mixture from heat. Add lemon juice and stir.

3. Mix with cooked spaghetti and top with Parmesan.

*Substitute 1/4 cup dry white wine for lemon juice, cook an additional 1-2 minutes, then add parsley. Remove from heat and add 1 tbsp butter, and allow to just melt before serving.*

CURLY PARSLEY

FLAT ITALIAN PARSLEY

## Olive Oil

**Cold pressed:** The best way to press olives; no chemicals are used; produces a natural level of low acidity.

**Extra virgin:** Cold-pressed result of the first pressing; 1 percent acidity; finest and fruitiest; in general, the deeper the color, the more intense the olive flavor.

**Light olive oil:** "Light" refers to color and fragrance, not the number of calories; different filtration process yields an oil with a higher "smoke point" (therefore, good for high-heat frying).

# Spaghetti with Lentils

   50 minutes

1 small yellow onion, chopped
2 tbsp oil
1/2 cup lentils, rinsed
2 cups water + 1-1/2 chicken bouillon cubes
1/2 cup crushed tomatoes
salt and black pepper to taste
3 tbsp grated Parmesan cheese

1. Just after you've put the spaghetti water on, heat the oil in a medium saucepot or skillet over medium flame. Add the onion and sauté 2-3 minutes, until translucent. Add the lentils, pepper, water, bouillon cubes, and mix. Reduce flame to low and cover the pot. Cook 30-40 minutes, until lentils are tender. Add the tomatoes and salt, and mix. Remove from heat.

2. Add drained spaghetti to skillet along with the Parmesan.

# Spicy Tomato Sauce

    **20 minutes**

**2 tbsp olive oil**
**1 small yellow onion, chopped**
**2 cloves garlic, chopped**
**1/4 cup water**
**28-oz can crushed tomatoes**
**1/2 tsp salt**
**1/4 tsp black pepper**
**1/4 tsp red pepper flakes**
**pinch sugar**

1. Just before the spaghetti water comes to a boil, heat the oil in a medium skillet over medium flame and add the onion. Stir constantly for 1 minute, then add garlic and cook, stirring constantly, for 1-2 more minutes. Add tomatoes, water, salt, pepper, sugar, and red pepper flakes. Reduce flame to low and cook an additional 10-12 minutes, until sauce has thickened.

2. Serve over cooked spaghetti.

*After you've chopped the onion and garlic, cut 4 strips thawed bacon into small pieces and cook in large skillet over medium-low flame until bacon is well cooked, but not crisp. Remove bacon with a slotted spoon to a paper towel to drain, then sauté onion and garlic as directed, in the bacon fat (omit the oil) and continue step 1. Add bacon back to sauce just before serving.*

# Spaghetti with Cream Sauce

   **10 minutes**

**2 tbsp butter or margarine**
**2 tbsp flour**
**1 cup milk**
**1/2 tsp salt**
**1/2 tsp black pepper**
**1/4 tsp cayenne pepper**
**3 tbsp grated Parmesan cheese**

1. Ten minutes before spaghetti is cooked, melt the butter in a medium skillet over low flame and add flour, stirring constantly until it is well incorporated.

2. Add the milk, salt, pepper, and cayenne and with a wire whisk continue stirring until mixture is thick, about 30 seconds. Remove from heat.

3. Add drained cooked spaghetti to sauce and mix well; add Parmesan cheese and mix again. Serve and eat.

*Top each serving with 1 tbsp chopped scallions (green part only) or chives.*

# Spaghetti Baked with Cheddar Cheese

   **1 hour**

**1/2 lb spaghetti**
**1 cup milk**
**2-1/2 tbsp butter or margarine**
**2 tbsp flour**
**1-1/4 cups grated cheddar cheese**
**salt and black pepper to taste**

1. Break the spaghetti into thirds and cook as directed on p. 92.

2. While spaghetti is cooking, preheat oven to 350°F.

3. Butter a casserole dish or loaf pan, or an 8" x 3" disposable aluminum pan with 1/2 tbsp of the butter.

4. In a medium saucepot, melt the remaining butter over a low flame; add the flour and whisk to incorporate. Add the milk, salt, pepper, and 1 cup cheese, whisking constantly. Continue to stir constantly until the mixture has thickened and the cheese is melted.

5. Drain the cooked pasta and add it to the cheese sauce; mix well, then pour into buttered casserole dish, and top with the remaining cheese. Bake 20-25 minutes until top is golden and bubbly.

   **Two words:** Oven mitts.

 *Add 1/4 cup Pomi or crushed tomatoes and an additional tsp salt along with the cheese in step 4.*

## Hard Beats Soft Any Day of the Week

About ten years ago, fresh pasta started showing up in the refrigerator section of every supermarket. It looked so authoritative, with its mutedly elegant packaging and its expiration date, so authentic, and so, well, fresh. In truth, however, the only thing to recommend this so-called fresh pasta is the fact that it takes two minutes to cook. And the list of cons goes on and on: it's expensive; it's mushy; it's expensive; it probably sat in the warehouse for three weeks; it's expensive; it's expensive. Stick with the boxed stuff.

# Spaghetti with Peas and Bacon

    **15 minutes**

**4 strips bacon**
**1/2 box frozen peas**
**1/4 tsp white pepper**
**grated Parmesan cheese**

1. While the spaghetti water is boiling, let the bacon thaw and chop it into small pieces.
2. Cook the frozen peas (p. 44); drain and set aside.
3. Ten minutes before the spaghetti is cooked, cook the bacon in a medium skillet over a medium flame until it begins to get crisp. Add the peas and pepper and stir; remove from heat.
4. Pour over cooked, drained spaghetti and serve topped with Parmesan.

# Cold Spaghetti with Soy Sauce

    **15 minutes**

*A summer treat, but an acquired taste. Try it with Japanese buckwheat noodles, too.*

**1/2 cup or more soy sauce**
**1-2 trays of ice**

1. Divide soy sauce between two bowls.

2. Divide ice between two bowls.

3. When the spaghetti is cooked, drain and run under cold water until cool to the touch. Place over ice in bowls.

4. To eat, pick up a few spaghetti strands with your fork, dip in soy sauce, place in mouth. Mmmmmm . . . tasty.

 *Add 1 tbsp sesame oil to each bowl of soy sauce.*

# Spaghetti Carbonara

         **15 minutes**

**6 strips bacon**
**1 egg**
**black pepper to taste**
**1/4 cup grated Parmesan cheese**

1. While the spaghetti water is boiling, fry the bacon in a medium skillet over low flame until crisp. Turn off heat, remove bacon from pan, and place on paper towels to drain. Save the bacon grease. When bacon has cooled, crumble it with your fingers into small pieces.

2. While the spaghetti is cooking, beat the egg until well-mixed.

3. Once spaghetti is drained, place back in pot and immediately add egg, mixing constantly with a fork until it is well incorporated and the egg has cooked itself onto the spaghetti. Add bacon grease, pepper, and Parmesan. Top with more Parmesan, if desired.

 *Add 4 tbsp chopped fresh parsley in step 3.*

# Spaghetti with Butter

   1 minute

**1/2 stick salted butter**

1.  While the spaghetti is cooking, melt butter in small sauce-pot over low flame. Don't let it burn. Remove from heat.
2.  Pour melted butter over cooked, drained spaghetti, and mix well before eating.

 *Don't make this; make something else.*

# Spaghetti with White Beans and Carrots

   25 minutes

**2 carrots, peeled and chopped**
**1/3 cup olive oil**
**2 cloves garlic, chopped**
**1 tbsp fresh rosemary, chopped, or 1 tsp dried**
**1 large fresh tomato or 2 canned tomatoes, chopped**
**15-oz can white kidney beans, rinsed and drained**
**3/4 tsp + pinch salt**
**1/4 tsp black pepper**
**grated Parmesan cheese**

1. While the spaghetti water is boiling, place the carrots in a saucepot with a pinch of salt and cover with cold water. Bring to a boil over medium-high heat and cook until tender, 7-10 minutes.

2. Heat the oil in a skillet over medium flame and add the garlic and rosemary. Stirring constantly, cook 1 minute, then add tomatoes and stir to mix. Add the beans, carrots, salt, and pepper and cook until heated through. Remove from flame. Add cooked, drained spaghetti and mix well. Serve topped with grated Parmesan.

# Spaghetti with Oregano

     15 minutes

**1/3 cup olive oil**
**4 cloves garlic, chopped**
**2 tbsp fresh oregano, leaves only, or 2 tsp dried**
**3/4 tsp salt**
**1/4 tsp black pepper**
**grated Parmesan cheese**

1. Ten minutes before the spaghetti is cooked, heat oil in medium skillet over medium flame, add garlic, and cook 3-5 minutes, until it begins to brown. Add oregano, salt and pepper. Mix well. Remove from flame.

2. Add cooked, drained spaghetti to oil and oregano mixture and toss to combine. Top with Parmesan and serve.

## Generic vs. Name Brands

There are several generic-brand items that pale in comparison to their famous-name counterparts. Scoff at our findings if you will, but don't say we didn't warn you.

1. Raisin bran: For some reason, the flakes in every generic brand we've tried taste like toasted styrofoam.

2. Frozen dinners: Think back to your grade school cafeteria days: Remember brown string beans and green mystery meat? Same color-confusion applies here.

3. Pasta: All the glueyness of unbaked cookie dough, none of the charm.

# Leftover Spaghetti Lo Mein

   **20 minutes**

1 cup leftover spaghetti
1/2 cup chicken, pork, or beef, cut into small
   cubes
1-1/2 tbsp butter or margarine
1/4 tsp garlic powder
1/4 tsp black pepper
1 tbsp soy sauce

1. In a medium skillet, melt 1 tbsp of butter or margarine over a medium flame. Add meat, garlic powder and pepper, and cook until browned all over, 3-5 minutes.

2. Add 1/2 tbsp soy sauce to the meat and stir will to coat. Add spaghetti, the remaining butter and soy sauce, and mix well to combine. Cook 30 seconds, until butter is melted. Eat while it's hot.

 *Add 1/4 cup bean sprouts with spaghetti in step 2.*

# Chicken Soup with Leftover Spaghetti

   **5 minutes**

1/2 - 1 cup leftover cooked spaghetti
1/2 cup canned chicken broth or 1/2 chicken
   bouillon cube plus 1/2 cup water

1. Place the spaghetti in a medium saucepot with broth or bouillon cube and water. Heat over medium flame until spaghetti is heated through and/or bouillon cube has dissolved.

 *Add black pepper to taste. Top with grated cheese.*

# Noodles (The Real Thing)

No, pasta isn't the only kind of noodle we know. Here are the rest, with special attention paid to a novice chef's best friend, ramen.

# Buttered Noodles

   **25 minutes**

**1/2 lb egg noodles (you decide on the size)**
**medium saucepot filled with water**
**1 tsp + 1/4 tsp salt**
**1/4 tsp black pepper**
**4 tbsp butter or margarine**

1. Bring the water to a boil. Add 1 tsp salt and the noodles. Stir with a fork to ensure noodles aren't sticking together.

2. Read package directions for cooking time and at the appropriate moment, drain noodles into a colander. Place back in stockpot and add butter, remaining 1/4 tsp salt, and pepper. Stir until butter melts and ingredients are well combined.

 *Add 1 tbsp sesame seeds with the butter, salt, and pepper in step 2.*

*The Book of Ramen*, by Ron Konzak

# Egg Noodles with Zucchini

      **25 minutes**

**1/2 lb egg noodles**
**medium saucepot filled with water and 1 tsp salt**
**2 small or 1 medium zucchini**
**2 cloves garlic**
**4 tbsp olive oil**
**1/2 tsp salt**
**1/4 tsp black pepper**
**grated Parmesan cheese (optional)**

1. While the water for the noodles is boiling, wash the zucchini and chop into dime-sized pieces. Set aside.

2. Chop the garlic and set aside.

3. Follow step 1 for Buttered Noodles (p. 109).

4. Heat the oil in a medium-sized skillet over medium flame, add the zucchini, garlic, 1tsp salt, and pepper and cook, stirring constantly, for 2-3 minutes, until zucchini begins to brown slightly. Remove from flame.

5. Drain the noodles when they're cooked, return them to the pot, and add the zucchini mixture. Mix well, place on plates, and top with Parmesan if desired.

## Ramen

You love it, you like it, but you're sick of it. Behold: Five ways to liven up that confounded ramen. But first, a rule of thumb: generic brands suck. Then again, so do most of those big-name brands you find in the supermarket. If you live near a health food store, buy your ramen there.

# Ramen Egg Drop

   15 minutes

*Same premise as Egg Drop Soup (p. 62), but the noodles make this more of a meal.*

**3-oz package chicken ramen**
**1 egg**

1. Make ramen noodles according to package directions.
2. While the ramen is cooking, crack egg into a bowl—try not to get any bits of shell in there—and beat with a fork.
3. After you've added the spice packet to the noodles, put the pot back on the stove over high flame until broth boils again. Then add egg in a slow, steady stream, mixing the broth constantly with a fork as you do so.
4. Remove from heat and place in a bowl. Eat with a large spoon, a fork, and a bib, if necessary.

# Ramen with Peas

   15 minutes

**3-oz package chicken or miso ramen**
**1/4 cup frozen peas**

1. Follow directions on package; add peas to the water at the same time you add the noodles. Continue preparation as directed on package, adding spice packet at appropriate moment.

# Ramen with Leftover Meat

   20 minutes

**3-oz package chicken, beef, or pork Ramen, determined by what kind of meat you've got**
**1/4 cup leftover chicken, beef, or pork**

1. Slice leftover meat into bite-sized pieces.
2. Make ramen according to package directions; add meat to water along with noodles. Add spice packet as package indicates.

# Ramen with Yogurt and Curry

     🕐 15 minutes

**3-oz package chicken or miso ramen**
**2 tbsp yogurt**
**1/2 tsp curry powder**

1. Cook ramen according to package directions and drain. Place in a bowl.
2. To the noodles, add half of the accompanying spice packet, the yogurt and curry, and mix well to incorporate.

# Sesame Ramen

     🕐 15 minutes

**3-oz package miso ramen**
**1 tbsp sesame oil**
**1 tsp sesame seeds**
**1 clove finely chopped garlic**
**1/4 cup chopped cucumbers or chopped red peppers**

1. Make ramen according to package directions. Drain and place in bowl.
2. Add sesame oil, garlic, sesame seeds, half of the accompanying spice packet, and cucumbers or peppers and mix well to combine.

# Macaroni and Cheese

There are a lot of brands out there but for some reason, we always reach for the Kraft. Maybe it's the toxic orange color that we find so inviting, or the too tangy flavor of completely artificial processed cheese. Whatever the reason, we don't seem to be able to get enough of it. Below, two ways—vegetarian and non—to make it even more palatable than it is to begin with.

# Macaroni and Cheese with Tomato and Tabasco

    **30 minutes**

**1 box Kraft Macaroni and Cheese**
**1/3 cup crushed tomatoes**
**2 pinches salt**
**1/4 tsp black pepper**
**4 dashes or more Tabasco**

1. While the water is boiling for the macaroni, place the crushed tomatoes, salt, pepper, and Tabasco in a medium saucepot, stir, and heat over medium-low flame. When it's hot, remove from heat, cover, and set aside.

2. Once macaroni is cooked and drained, place it back in the pot, add tomato sauce, and follow directions for adding cheese sauce. Mix well and serve.

# Macaroni and Cheese with Ground Beef

    30 minutes

**1 box Kraft Macaroni and Cheese**
**1 tsp garlic powder**
**2 tsp Worcestershire sauce**
**1/2 lb ground beef**

1. While the water for the macaroni is boiling, heat a medium skillet over medium-high flame. Add ground beef, Worcestershire, and garlic powder and cook, stirring constantly with a spoon to break up the pieces, for 3-5 minutes, until beef is well browned all over. Remove from flame and drain in a colander. Set aside.

2. Once the macaroni is cooked, drain and place back in the pot. Add ground beef, and follow package instructions for making cheese sauce. Mix well and serve.

# 8

# *Dead Animals: Meat and Fish*

Once upon a time, we tried to be vegetarian. We never felt better: So light, so energetic, so PC. And our finances were healthier than they had been in years. The only problem was that every couple of weeks we'd get a craving for a big, bloody steak and, being first and foremost self-indulgent, we just couldn't resist. Whatever your carnal (or pescal) urge, this chapter seeks to satisfy.

# Beef

Beef is by far the most versatile meat; you can fry it, grill it, broil it, boil it, and guess what? It still tastes like beef.

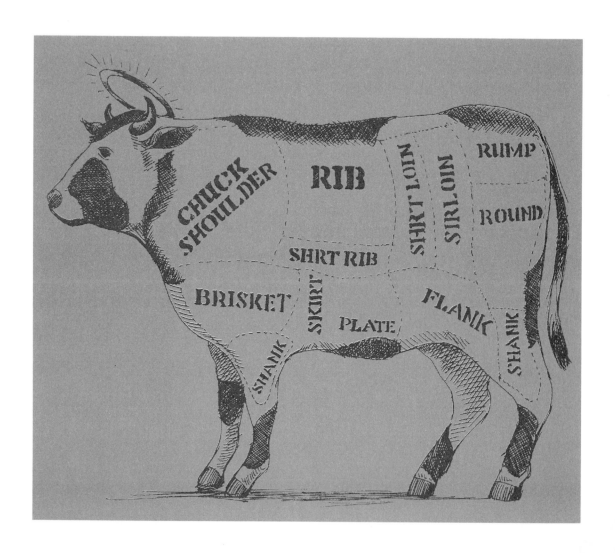

# The Standard Hamburger

   20 minutes

**1 lb ground beef, the leaner the better**
**2 tbsp Worcestershire sauce**
**2 hamburger buns (optional)**

1. Wash your hands.

2. Place the ground beef in a bowl, and divide into two halves. Knead each half until the meat holds together; work into a ball, then flatten into patties.

3. Heat a medium skillet over a medium flame. Add the burgers and reduce flame to low. Sprinkle with 1 tbsp Worcestershire sauce. Cook 5-7 minutes, until bottom is well-browned.

4. Flip burgers with a spatula and sprinkle with remaining Worcestershire. Cook an additional 5-10 minutes, until a knife inserted into the center of the burgers reveals that they are cooked to desired doneness.

5. Place on plates or hamburger buns and serve with toppings of your choice.

# The Complicated Hamburger

   30 minutes

**1 lb ground beef**
**1 small onion, chopped**
**1 tbsp oil**
**1/2 tsp garlic powder**
**1 tsp dried oregano**
**pinch salt**
**pinch black pepper**
**2 tbsp Worcestershire sauce**
**2 hamburger buns (optional)**

1. Heat the oil in a small skillet over a medium flame; add the onion, salt, and pepper and cook, stirring constantly, for 2-3 minutes, until onion is translucent. Remove with slotted spoon and place in bowl.

2. Open ground beef and place in bowl; add onion, garlic powder, dried oregano, and proceed with steps 3-5 of Standard Hamburgers.

# Hamburger Toppings

*Sometimes, a plain old hamburger just doesn't cut it. Additional toppings will liven it up.*

   **Varies**

**Cheese:** Thinly slice your choice of cheddar, American, Jack, etc. Place on top of burger after you've flipped it and it's cooked about 5 minutes on second side. Cover skillet with lid so the cheese melts.

**Mushrooms:** Wash and slice 4 mushrooms. Once you've put the burger on to cook, heat 1 tbsp of butter or margarine and 1 tbsp oil in a small skillet over medium flame. Add mushrooms, pinch salt, pinch black pepper, and cook 5 minutes, stirring constantly, until mushrooms are wilted. Remove from skillet and serve on top of cooked burger.

**Onions:** Peel a small onion and slice it into thin rounds. Once you've put the burger on to cook, heat 2 tbsp of oil in a skillet over medium flame and add onion, pinch salt, pinch pepper and cook 5-7 minutes, stirring constantly, until the onion begins to brown. Serve on top of the cooked burger.

**Bacon:** Once you've put the burger on to cook, heat a small skillet over medium heat and lay 2 strips bacon flat across it. Cook, drain on paper towels, and serve on top of cooked burger.

## A Lesson in Deep-Frying

The Worst Kitchen Disaster Story We've Ever Heard "The guys I was living with in St. Paul liked to deep-fry things. One of them got home from work one night and turned on the stove to heat up the oil, but left the cover on the pot—a big no-no. The phone rang and he talked for a long time, and when he hung up, he realized he still had the pot on the stove. He went into the kitchen and knew it was trouble: the oil, because it was covered and there was no air getting in, was beyond the boiling point. (continued on next page)

# Tacos

   **60 minutes**

**1 lb ground beef**
**8 taco shells**
**1 packet taco seasoning mix**
**1 large tomato**
**4 iceberg lettuce leaves**
**4 oz cheddar cheese**
**sour cream**
**guacamole (p. 187)**
**salsa, jarred or homemade (p. 188)**

1. Make the guacamole, place in bowl, and set aside.

2. Make the salsa, if you're making it, and set aside; otherwise, place jarred stuff in a bowl.

3. Brown the ground beef in a large skillet over a medium flame. Drain. Add taco seasoning mix and continue cooking as directed on the package (about 20 minutes).

4. While that's going on, preheat the oven to 350°F; core, wash, and dice the tomato; wash, dry, and shred the lettuce; and grate the cheese. Put all these ingredients, plus the sour cream, in separate bowls and place on table.

5. Place the taco shells in the oven until crisp, about 5 minutes. Remove from oven.

6. Divide meat mixture evenly between taco shells and place on plates. Add toppings as desired, along with Tabasco.

# Split-Fried Hot Dogs

   15 minutes

**4 beef hot dogs**
**2 tbsp butter or margarine**
**garlic salt**
**dried oregano**
**4 hot dog buns (optional)**

1. With a sharp knife, split the hot dogs lengthwise and open them up, but don't cut them so far that they split completely in half.

2. In a large skillet, melt 1 tbsp butter over medium heat until it begins to sizzle. Add hot dogs, flat side down, and sprinkle with garlic salt and oregano. Cook 3-5 minutes, until they're browned on the bottom and are beginning to curl up at the edges.

3. Flip hot dogs with a fork, add remaining tbsp butter to skillet, and sprinkle again with garlic salt and oregano, then press them down firmly to the pan with the back of the fork so they cook evenly all over. Cook an additional 2-4 minutes, until well browned on the second side.

4. Eat with mustard, with or without buns.

 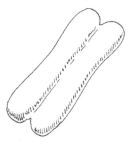

He picked up the pot and started moving it toward the sink, which was full of ice-cold water and dirty dishes. The handle broke off and the pot fell into the sink of water. The whole thing exploded, covering the entire kitchen with flaming oil. When I got home, I walked into the kitchen and it was black—floors, walls, ceiling. And it was a mess, dripping with water from the fire department hosing it down. Eventually my roommate got home from the hospital —his hairline had moved back an inch and he had severely burned his hands (he had to wear cotton gloves for weeks). I doubt he ever deep-fried again—I think he just went to a lot of restaurants."

Andy B.,
University of Minnesota

# Meatloaf

  **2 hours**

**3 lbs ground beef  (or pick up a meatloaf pack at the supermarket, which contains beef, pork, and veal)**

**2 eggs**

**1 tsp salt**

**3 tbsp Worcestershire sauce**

**1-1/2 tsp black pepper**

**2 tsp garlic powder**

**1/2 cup breadcrumbs**

**1 tbsp butter or margarine**

1. Wash your hands.

2. Preheat oven to 350°F.

3. Grease a loaf pan with the butter.

4. Mix all the remaining ingredients together in a large bowl with your hands (be sure to remove the eggs from their shells first). Place in loaf pan and pat it down so that it covers evenly.

5. Place on center rack of oven and bake for 1-1/2 hours. To test for doneness, insert a knife into the center of the loaf. If it's still pink, let cook an additional 10-15 minutes before checking again, inserting knife into a different spot.

6. Remove from oven and allow to sit at room temperature for 5-10 minutes before cutting up and serving.

*Chop up a small onion and cook it in a small skillet over medium flame in 1 tbsp oil for 5 minutes, until translucent. Add to ground meat in step 4. Top meatloaf with 2 tbsp tomato paste or ketchup before placing in oven.*

# Semi-Shepherd's Pie

   30 minutes

**1 lb ground beef**
**3 baking potatoes**
**2 tbsp Worcestershire sauce**
**1 tsp garlic powder**
**1/2 tsp + 1/2 tsp salt**
**1/4 tsp + 1/4 tsp black pepper**
**3 tbsp butter or margarine**
**1/2 cup milk**

1. Wash and peel the potatoes, and cut them into 2-inch pieces. Place them in a medium-sized pot and cover with water. Bring to a boil over high heat, then reduce flame to medium and cook about 20 minutes, until tender. Drain and place back in pot over very low flame with butter, milk, 1/2 tsp salt, and 1/4 tsp pepper. Mash until smoothish with a potato masher, adding more milk if necessary. Remove from heat.

2. While the potatoes are cooking, heat a medium skillet over a medium flame. Add ground beef, garlic powder, remaining salt and pepper, and Worcestershire; stir to break up pieces, and continue stirring often until beef is well browned all over, 3-5 minutes. Taste for seasoning and add more Worcestershire, if desired. Drain.

3. To serve: Divide the mashed potatoes evenly between two plates and top with ground beef.

"Eaten by Her Own Dinner," by Robin Hitchcock and the Egyptians

"5-Piece Chicken Dinner," by The Beastie Boys

# Beef Stew

   2-1/2 hours

**1-1/2 lbs cubed stewing beef**
**1/2 cup flour**
**1 tsp salt**
**1 tsp black pepper**
**2 tbsp olive oil or 1 tbsp vegetable oil**
**  + 1 tbsp butter**
**1 medium onion**
**2 cloves garlic**
**6 cloves**
**2 carrots**
**3 ribs celery**
**2 small baking potatoes**
**1/2 package frozen peas**
**2-1/2 cups water**
**2-1/2 chicken bouillon cubes (optional)**

1. Peel the onion and stud it with the cloves. Set aside.

2. Remove skin from the garlic. Set aside.

3. Place the flour, salt, and pepper in a medium-sized bowl and mix well to combine.

4. Heat the oil, or the oil and butter, in a medium-sized stockpot over a medium flame.

5. While the oil's heating, dredge the beef cubes in the flour mixture, making sure each cube is coated all over, then shake off excess. Add, carefully, to the oil in the stockpot along with the garlic cloves. As the beef browns, flip each cube over so that it browns on every side.  It'll take about 3 minutes per side.

6. Once the beef is browned all over, add the water and/or bouillon cubes, the onion and garlic, bring to a boil, then reduce flame to low (as low as you can go), and cover the pot with a lid. Stir occasionally (about every 15 minutes) with a wooden spoon, making sure that the meat doesn't stick and that there's ample liquid. Add more water (1/4 cup at a time), if necessary.

7. Peel the carrots and cut them into 2-inch pieces. Set aside. Wash the celery and cut into 2-inch pieces. Set aside. Peel the potatoes and cut them into 1-inch cubes. Set aside. Add to stew after it's been simmering for about 1-1/4 hours. Remember to keep stirring.

8. After 2 hours, the meat should be extremely tender. If it's not, add a little more water and cook a little longer, until the beef just falls right off the tines of a fork. Add the peas and cook an additional 15 minutes.

9. Serve with rice, or buttered noodles (p. 109). Stew actually tastes better the second and third days, so revel in leftovers.

*Fifty-Two Meatloaves*, by **Michael McLaughlin**

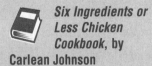
*Six Ingredients or Less Chicken Cookbook*, by **Carlean Johnson**

*Chilimania*, by **Herb & Chris Geltner**

CLOVE

CLOVE OF GARLIC

## Eating for Free

Nothing in the fridge? No money in your pocket? Then you need a way to eat for free, without getting arrested.

## Idea #1:

Call local art galleries to find out when they're having openings. You'll at least get a few cups of cheap white wine into you, guaranteed to take the edge off hunger pangs.
(Go to next page)

# Steak on the Stove

   **15 minutes**

**1 nice piece juicy looking steak; 1/2 lb is ample for 1 person**

**1/2 tsp salt**

1. Heat a heavy bottomed, medium-sized skillet over medium-high flame. Sprinkle pan with salt, then add steak. Reduce flame to medium and cook 5-7 minutes, until bottom is well browned.

2. Flip steak over with a fork and cook an additional 3-7 minutes, until bottom is browned and a cut in the center of the steak with a knife reveals that it's cooked as rare as you like it. Move from skillet to plate.

 *Press lots of freshly ground black pepper into steak on both sides while skillet is heating. Proceed from step 1.*

# Steak in the Broiler

   **15-20 minutes**

**1/2-1 lb steak**

1. Preheat broiler.

2. Place steak on tin foil and stick under broiler. Cook 5-7 minutes, until top is well browned. Flip over and cook an

additional 3-7 minutes (see step 2 of Steak on the Stove to check that it's cooked as you like it). Serve with Worcestershire or steak sauce, if desired.

*Mix together 2 tbsp olive oil, 2 tbsp red wine, and 2 tsp black pepper in a shallow baking dish; add steak and coat it all over with oil mixture. Cover with Saran Wrap and marinate in refrigerator for 1/2 to 1 hour. Leave it in same handy baking dish to broil.*

# Sloppy Joes

   **30 minutes**

*Just like you remember them from your grade school cafeteria.*

**1 lb ground beef**
**1 cup crushed tomatoes**
**1 package taco seasoning mix**
**2 toasted hamburger buns**

**3/4 cup water**
**2 tsp Worcestershire sauce**
**1 tsp garlic powder**
**4 dashes Tabasco sauce**

1.  Heat a large skillet over a medium flame. Add beef and stir constantly with a spoon to break it up. Cook about 3 minutes, until browned all over. Drain off the fat, add remaining ingredients (minus the buns), and mix well. Cook 10 more minutes, stirring often until sauce thickens.

2.  Serve over toasted hamburger buns.

**Eating for Free Idea #2:**

Visit the local gourmet supermarket or health food store where, frequently, samplings of new food products are offered in the aisles. Casually take a few tastes, browse around the store a little, come back and sample a little more. Continue until you get thrown out.
(Go to page 140)

# Betty Crocker au Gratin Potatoes with Ground Beef

*This recipe may or may not have been invented by Rob E. (University of Florida) who says, "Oh, man! Just thinking about them makes me want them right now." His directions for preparation:*

      **1 hour**

**1 box Betty Crocker au Gratin Potatoes**
**1/2 lb hamburger meat**
**1 tsp garlic powder**
**dash of salt**
**dash of pepper**
**dash of Cayenne pepper**

1. Take 1/2 lb hamburger meat, fry it up with some garlic powder, some salt, some pepper, maybe a little bit of Cayenne. Drain the meat.

2. Put the boxed potatoes in a baking dish, mix them up with the ground beef, and make them like they tell you on the box.

*If you like, top with breadcrumbs or, if you have Ritz crackers or Saltines, crush them and sprinkle on top.*

# Pork

Tender and succulent when prepared correctly, a pork chop is just the thing to feast upon come a frosty winter's night. Don't think you can prepare pig at a second's notice though, pork needs to cook quite a while to reach it's peak flavor, and to rid itself of germs. Try one of the following recipes when you've got a spare hour or two.

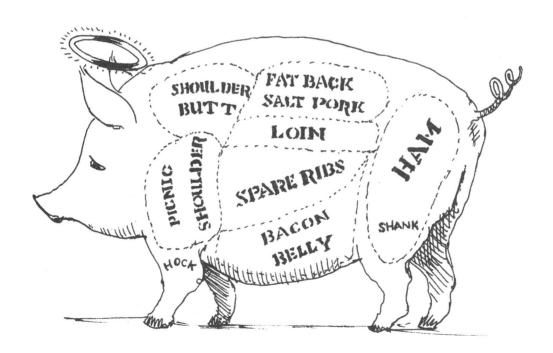

# Pork Chops with Celery and Onion

   **1-1/2 hours**

**1-1/2 lbs pork chops (boneless or center cut, 2-4 chops)**
**1-1/2 tbsp oil**
**2 cloves garlic**
**2 ribs celery**
**1 large onion**
**1 cup water + 1 chicken bouillon cube**
**1 tbsp dried thyme**
**2 tsp black pepper**

1.  Remove skin from garlic clove. Set aside.

2.  Wash and dice the celery. Set aside.

3.  Chop the onion. Set aside.

4.  In a medium skillet, heat the oil over a medium-high flame and add the pork chops and garlic. Sprinkle with 1/2 tbsp thyme and 1 tsp black pepper. Cook 2-3 minutes, until browned on the bottom. Flip over with a fork, sprinkle with remaining thyme and pepper, and cook an additional 1-2 minutes, until browned on the other side. Add celery, onion, water, and bouillon cube. Reduce flame to low and cover skillet.

5.  Cook 30 minutes, then flip pork chops over. Cook an additional 30-45 minutes, until pork chops are tender (they should also be white in the center). Place chops on two plates and top with celery/onion mixture. Serve with rice or buttered noodles (p. 109).

# Pork Chops with Apples

   1 hour and 15 minutes

**2 center cut pork chops**
**1/2 Granny Smith apple**
**1 tsp cinnamon**
**1/2 tsp allspice**
**1/2 tsp salt**
**1/2 tsp black pepper**

1. Preheat oven to 350°F.

2. Peel and core the apple half, and slice very thin.

3. Place pork chops in ovenproof dish, sprinkle with cinnamon, allspice, salt, and pepper, and top with apple slices.

4. Cover dish (with lid or tin foil), and place on center rack of oven. Cook for 1 hour (or longer, if necessary), until pork chops are tender and cooked through. Eat immediately.

## Spam

Spam, that wonderfully salty, fatty, ground pork shoulder and ham concoction, was invented in 1937 by Jay C. Hormel, the son of Hormel founder George Hormel, to use up surplus pork shoulder. Jay C. Hormel was a genius. By 1944, 5 billion cans of Spam had been produced, enough to circle the Earth twelve and a half times.

# Hot Sausages with Tomato and Onion

   **45 minutes**

**1 lb hot Italian sausage**
**6 ripe plum tomatoes, or 1 cup canned**
**1 small red onion**
**1 tbsp olive oil**
**1/4 tsp black pepper**

1. Wash the tomatoes, remove the cores, and chop. Set aside.

2. Chop the onion. Set aside.

3. Remove the casings from the sausages and cut into 1-inch pieces.

4. Heat the oil in a large skillet over a medium flame. Add sausages and brown slightly, about 1 minute. Add tomatoes and pepper, stir well and cook approximately 20 minutes, until the sausages are golden brown, and the juice from the tomatoes has thickened to make a sauce. Serve with rice or buttered noodles (p. 109).

## Poultry

There are so many varieties of poultry we hardly know where to begin. Even the most poorly stocked of supermarkets will yield chicken and turkey cutlets, breasts, drumsticks, thighs, variety packs, and whole birds. Better stores will also carry other birds (i.e., hens, capons, ducks) in whole form. We've come up with a few simple recipes here to get you started.

# Lemon Cutlets

   20 minutes

**1 chicken or turkey cutlet, about 1/3 lb,
   pounded very thin**
**1/2 tbsp butter or margarine**
**1/2 tbsp oil**
**1/2 lemon**
**salt and black pepper to taste**

1. Rinse the cutlet under cold water and pat it dry with a
   paper towel.

2. Heat the butter and oil in a medium skillet over a medium-
   high flame. Add the cutlet and increase flame to high.
   Squirt with juice of 1/4 lemon and sprinkle with salt and
   pepper. Cook 2 minutes, until top of cutlet begins to turn
   white around the edges.

3. Flip the cutlet and sprinkle with remaining lemon juice,
   salt, and pepper. Cook until bottom is golden, about 2
   more minutes, and make an incision in the center of the
   cutlet with a knife to make sure it's cooked white all the
   way through. Remove from skillet, turn off gas, eat cutlet.

*Add 1 clove garlic, skin removed, at the begin-
ning of step 2. Discard before serving cutlet.*

*Sprinkle cooked cutlet with 1 tsp chopped,
fresh parsley.*

*Serve a lemon wedge on the side. Squeeze
over cooked cutlet.*

## Anyone for Turkey?

"The turkey farmers were novices. Before Thanksgiving they'd butchered their birds in an unheated shed, and all the blood froze in their bodies and turned them purple. The local butcher came out for a look. He suggested that the birds be kept in a warm bath for a few days—maybe that would loosen things up and turn them pink. The bath they used was ours. For almost two weeks we had these bumpy blue carcasses floating in the tub."

from
*This Boy's Life*,
by Tobias Wolff

# Cutlet with Vinegar

   **20 minutes**

**1 chicken or turkey cutlet, about 1/2 lb, pounded very thin**
**1/4 cup flour**
**1 tsp salt**
**1/2 tsp black pepper**
**2 tbsp olive oil**
**3 tbsp balsamic vinegar**

1. Rinse the cutlet under cold water and pat dry with a paper towel.

2. On a small plate, mix the flour with the salt and pepper and combine well.

3. Heat the oil in a medium skillet over a medium-high flame.

4. Dredge the cutlet in the flour mixture making sure both sides are adequately covered and shake off excess. Place cutlet in skillet.

5. Cook cutlet 3-4 minutes, until bottom is golden. Flip. Cook an additional 2-3 minutes, until cooked through. Add vinegar to skillet and swirl around the pan. Flip cutlet again and cook another 10 seconds, so that it is completely coated with vinegar. Serve.

# Chicken Curry

    45 minutes

1 lb chicken meat (you decide on dark or white), cut into bite-sized pieces
3 tbsp oil
1 medium onion
2 cloves garlic
1 tbsp grated fresh ginger (optional)
1 tbsp curry powder
1/2 tsp turmeric (optional)
1 bay leaf

1/2 tsp ground coriander
1/4 tsp cayenne pepper
6 cloves
1/2 tsp cinnamon
1/4 tsp allspice (optional)
1/2 tsp black pepper
1 tbsp tomato paste
1 tsp brown sugar
1 cup water + 1 chicken bouillon cube

1. Chop the onion and garlic. Set aside.

2. In a small skillet, heat 1 tbsp oil over a high flame, add all the spices, but not the salt, mix well into a paste, and remove from flame. Set aside.

3. Heat the remaining 2 tbsp oil in a large skillet over a medium flame, add the onion, and cook 2 minutes. Add the garlic and ginger and cook an additional minute, stirring constantly.

4. Add the chicken pieces to the skillet and cook, about 5 minutes, until all the pieces are cooked white all over. Add the water, salt, sugar, spice mixture, and tomato paste, mix well, and lower flame to medium-low. Cook approximately 20 minutes, until liquid has thickened to a sauce and chicken is cooked through. Serve over rice.

 *Add 1/4 cup raisins just before removing from flame. Serve over basmati rice.*

# Baked Chicken Two Ways

Baking a chicken's really easy; we wouldn't lie to you about this. A 3-pound chicken will serve two to four people, depending on how hungry they are. Chicken cooks at about twenty minutes per pound, so figure on at least an hour for a three pounder. The easiest way to know if a chicken's done is to push down on a drumstick and feel if it's about ready to fall off the carcass. If it is, you're definitely safe. The skin will also be a handsome, chestnut brown color.

If you prefer a more sophisticated method of poultry testing, after about an hour, cut a slit into the chicken skin where the drumstick meets the carcass. If the juices running out of the slit are clear, it's cooked; if they're red (i.e., bloody), the chicken needs more baking. Check 10 to 20 minutes later by making a slit in the other drumstick. We promise, this is easy. It's also economical; the leftover meat is great for chicken sandwiches. Use the whole darn carcass to make chicken soup (even easier than baking the chicken in the first place).

# Baked Chicken #1

   1 hour and 15 minutes

**3 lb chicken**
**salt**
**black pepper**
**curry powder**

1. Preheat the oven to 350°F.

2. Take the chicken out of the package, remove the innards, and rinse the bird under cold water (don't forget to rinse out the cavity). Dry on paper towels and place on roasting rack inside baking pan (you can also use a disposable aluminum pan).

3. Sprinkle chicken all over—that is, top side, bottom side, under the arm pits, over the wings—with salt, pepper, and curry powder. Try to do this with some eye to even-handedness.

4. Place chicken on center rack of the oven and bake approximately 1 hour (see intro to Baked Chicken, left).

5. Remove from oven and carve up as best you can with a sharp knife and a fork. Oven mitts are crucial.

## Eating for Free (continued)

### Idea #3:

Look indecisive at the supermarket deli counter. When they ask, "Can I help you," babble something about a special kind of ham or cheese you had at a restaurant, and ask to taste a few of the items, so you can figure it out. After you've filled up a bit, announce, annoyed, that they don't have what you're looking for and beat a hasty retreat.
(Go to next page)

# Baked Chicken #2

   **1 hour and 15 minutes**

**3 lb chicken**
**1 lemon**
**salt**
**black pepper**
**1/4 cup olive oil**

1. Follow steps 1 and 2 of Baked Chicken #1.

2. Cut lemon in half and squeeze all over chicken. Sprinkle with salt and pepper, then pour oil into your hand and pat onto the chicken skin.

3. Proceed with steps 3 and 4 of Baked Chicken #1.

# Chicken Soup from Leftover Baked Chicken

   3-1/2 hours

carcass of 1 leftover baked chicken (for best
   results, there should be some meat left on
   the bones)

| | |
|---|---|
| **2 carrots** | **1 bay leaf** |
| **3 ribs celery** | **peel of 1 lemon** |
| **1 medium onion** | **salt to taste** |
| **10-15 black peppercorns** | |

1. Remove any remaining skin from the chicken. Place in a large stockpot.

2. Wash and peel the carrots, break them in half, and place them in the stockpot.

3. Wash the celery ribs, break them in half, and add to stockpot.

4. Peel the onion and add to stockpot.

5. Add the lemon peel, bay leaf, and peppercorns.

6. Add enough cold water to cover the chicken carcass. Place on stove over high heat and bring to a boil. Reduce flame to low, cover the pot, and cook for about 3 hours, until the broth tastes like broth.

7. Place a colander over a large bowl and strain the soup into it. Pick out the vegetables and bones from the colander and discard. Place chicken meat into the soup and season to taste with salt.

   **To store:** Keep covered in the refrigerator, if you plan to use within four days. Otherwise, place in sealed plastic container and store in freezer until ready to use.

   **To eat:** Place soup in pot and heat up over medium-low flame.

## Eating for Free Idea #4:

Sneak food out of a party/reception. For this ploy to be effective, you must arrive with a knapsack and a stash of zip-lock bags. If you're lucky, the party will be so hopping, no one will notice how many times you come back for "seconds."

# Leftover Chicken Salad

    **15 minutes**

**1-1/2 cups leftover cooked chicken**
**1/4 cup diced celery**
**2 tbsp mayonnaise**
**2 tbsp oil**
**1/2 tsp salt**
**1/4 tsp black pepper**

1.  Remove skin from chicken and dice into bite-sized pieces.
    Place in medium-sized bowl and add celery.

2.  In a small bowl, combine mayo with oil, salt, and pepper
    and mix to combine. Add to chicken/celery mixture and
    mix well. Serve as is, on a bed of lettuce, or on toast.

  *Add 1 tsp curry powder to mayo in step 2.*

# Fish

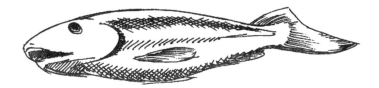

There's white-fleshed fish, like trout, sole, and bass, and there's red fleshed fish, like snapper and salmon. How you cook a fish depends less on its color than on the way it's cut: steaks (thick slabs sliced from the fish widthwise) work best if you broil them; fillets cook quickly on top of the stove; and whole fish are best when baked or poached.

FILLET

STEAK CUT

We really don't recommend purchasing fish at the supermarket—no way to check for nasty ammonia odors—so if it's fish you desire, off to the fish monger with you. No matter what you buy, it'll be relatively expensive, but one way to economize is to pick out a whole fish in the $4.00 - $6.00 per pound range (like bluefish or sea bass), tell the monger-in-residence you want to end up with about 3/4 of a

## How to Cook a Fish in the Dishwasher

You think we're making this up? Think again. This method of dishwasher poaching comes to us, thirdhand, from a bona fide chef (that is, someone who actually gets paid to prepare food). So the next time mom comes back from one of her fishing jaunts with too many bass and insists you take one home with you, subject it to this little experiment: Wrap one whole fish in Saran Wrap; make sure Saran Wrap is well sealed. Place fish on bottom rack of dishwasher. Do not, we repeat, do not add detergent. Shut and lock dishwasher, set water temperature to "hot," and turn on to regular wash. Once the dishwasher has run its cycle, pull out fish and poke at it with your finger: If it feels firm, it's cooked. If it still feels a little squishy, run it through another short wash. Unwrap fish from Saran Wrap. Eat at your own risk.

pound (sufficient for two people), then let him clean it and fillet it. What you'll take home are two pieces of boneless fish with the skin still on, which'll be a lot cheaper than buying two already-cleaned fillets with the skin off.

# Easy Stove-Top Fish

   10 minutes

**2 fillets of your choice, like bass, trout, blue-fish**
**2 tbsp butter or margarine**
**1 lemon**
**salt and black pepper**

1. Melt 1 tbsp butter in a large skillet over medium-high heat. Add the fillets, skin side down, and squeeze juice of half a lemon over them. Sprinkle with salt and pepper. Cook 2-4 minutes, until the fish begins to turn white around the top edge. Flip over with a spatula.

2. Squeeze juice of remaining half lemon over fish, sprinkle with more salt and pepper, and cook an additional 2-3 minutes, until fish is flaky and white all over.

3. Remove from heat and place on plates. Serve with additional lemon, if desired, and eat it while it's hot. The skin isn't bad for you, but we don't recommend you eat it; it'll peel away easily from the fish as you go.

# Broiled Fish Steaks

   1 hour and 15 minutes

**2 fish steaks of your choice like salmon,
  shark, or swordfish**
**4 tbsp olive oil**
**juice of 1 lemon**
**1/2 tsp black pepper**

1. In an ovenproof dish, mix the olive oil, lemon juice, and pepper. Add fish steaks, then flip over so that the marinade covers both sides. Cover with Saran Wrap and place in refrigerator for 1 hour.

2. Preheat broiler.

3. Remove fish from fridge, remove Saran Wrap, and place fish, dish and all, under broiler. Cook about 5 minutes, until top begins to turn golden, then flip and cook an additional 3-5 minutes, until a knife inserted into the center of the steaks reveals that they are cooked through. Fish should also feel consistently firm under the pressure of your little fingers.

4. Remove fish from broiler.

## To Sushi Or Not to Sushi

The puffer, or fugu, as it is known in Japan, is the world's deadliest sea creature. With a toxin 275 times more poisonous than cyanide, it paralyzes its victims for several hours before they die. Although the Japanese government has outlawed its sale, sushi made from selected portions of the fugu is highly prized by renegade gourmets. Improperly prepared fugu, however, will do a lot more than upset your stomach!

# Tuna Steaks

**1 hour and 15 minutes**

**4 tuna steaks**
**4 tbsp olive oil**
**1 tbsp + 1 tsp soy sauce**
**1-1/2 tsp grated fresh ginger**
**1 tsp dry mustard or wasabi powder**
**lots and lots of freshly ground black pepper**

1. Mix the olive oil, soy sauce, ginger, and mustard or wasabi in a shallow dish. Add tuna steaks and flip over, making sure they're well covered with marinade on both sides. Cover with Saran Wrap and place in the refrigerator for 45 minutes.

2. Remove tuna from fridge. Place lots and lots of freshly ground black pepper on a plate, place tuna steaks over them, then flip; steaks should be well covered with pepper, and to make sure it sticks, press the pepper into the fish with your fingers.

3. Heat a heavy-bottomed skillet over a high flame.  Add tuna and cook 2-3 minutes, until golden on the bottom. Flip over and cook an additional 2-3 minutes. Tuna should be well-seared on the outside, nice and pink on the inside. If you prefer it well done, cook almost 5 minutes per side. Let it sit for about 5 minutes before eating to let the juices settle, then dig in.

# Shellfish

Our favorite is lobster, the bigger the better. Don't even bother with the melted butter, just wrap us up in a bib, give us some nutcrackers, and get out of our way. But to be honest, we've never met a shellfish we wouldn't eat: oysters, clams, mussels, crab, shrimp, we love 'em all. Two words to the cautious: iodine poisoning. The more shellfish you eat in one sitting, the better your chances of experiencing this unfortunate and, yes, potentially fatal condition. Eat shellfish in moderation. A few more words to the brave: Leave the oyster shucking to the professionals. We know what we're talking about, and we have the scars to prove it. And that old maxim your granny told you about, you know the one—Oysters R in Season—applies to all shellfish and means, quite simply, that shellfish should only be eaten in months that have the letter "r" in them.

# Shrimp Cocktail

   **20 minutes**

*We know the combination of cocktail sauce ingredients sounds revolting, but there's nothing like a shrimp cocktail to please a date.*

**1/2 lb medium shrimp, peeled and deveined (p. 150)**
**1/2 cup jarred salsa**
**1/2 cup ketchup**
**dash Tabasco**
**1 tbsp horseradish**

1. Bring a medium saucepot of water to boil over high flame. Add shrimp and cook, 1-2 minutes, until all the shrimp have just turned pink. Drain into a colander and run under cold water until cool. Pat dry with paper towels and set aside.

2. Mix the remaining ingredients in a medium-sized bowl. Place bowl on a large plate, surround it with shrimp, and eat by picking up one shrimp at a time with your fingers, a toothpick, or a fork, and dipping in cocktail sauce.

# Shrimp Salad

   15 minutes

**1/2 lb medium shrimp, peeled and deveined (p. 150)**
**1/4 cup Italian dressing, mustard variation (p. 82)**
**2 tbsp mayonnaise**
**10 lettuce leaves, washed and dried**

1. Follow step 1 of Shrimp Cocktail.
2. In a small bowl, combine dressing and mayo with a small whisk. Pour over shrimp and mix well to combine.
3. Arrange lettuce leaves on two plates and top with shrimp salad.

*Arrange sliced cucumbers, avocado wedges, chopped tomatoes, or other vegetables of your choice around shrimp salad. Double recipe for Italian dressing and mayo combination; use half as directed above and pour the other half over vegetables.*

## Shrimp Cleaning 101

You don't have to peel and clean shrimp before you cook them, although taking this preliminary step allows you to avoid immersing your fingers in sauce and making a real mess. To clean: Hold shrimp gently in one hand and snap off tail with the other hand; pull. If you're lucky, the intestine will exit the shrimp as you pull the tail. Remove the rest of the shell by peeling it away from the feelers. If the intestine didn't come out with the tail, remove it either by pulling it out from the neck, or by making a shallow incision along the rounded back of the shrimp with a knife and scooping out.

# Spicy Shrimp Soup

        35 minutes

*This recipe requires that you use all fresh ingredients, no substitutions allowed. It's a bit fancy, we know, but you've bought shrimp, after all. If you make this for your mother when she comes to visit, she will buy you lots of presents.*

**12 medium shrimp, peeled and deveined (see left)**
**1 medium ripe tomato, cored and cut into 8 wedges**
**6 cloves garlic, chopped**
**2 tbsp olive oil**
**1 tbsp chopped fresh basil, leaves only**
**2 tbsp chopped fresh cilantro, leaves only**
**juice of 1 lime**
**1/4 tsp red pepper flakes**
**2 cups water + 2 fish bouillon cubes**

1. Boil the shrimp as per instructions for Shrimp Cocktail (p. 148), drain, and set aside.

2. In a small stockpot, heat the oil over medium flame, add the garlic and cook 2-3 minutes, until it browns. Add the water and bouillon cubes, and the red pepper flakes. Reduce flame to medium-low and cook until bouillon cubes have dissolved.

3. Add the tomatoes and the shrimp and cook an additional 1-2 minutes, until everything is warmed through. Remove from heat.

4. Squeeze the lime—1/2 into each of two bowls—and divide basil and cilantro between same two bowls. Then divide the shrimp and tomatoes evenly between the bowls and ladle the fish stock on top.

# Steamers

      20 minutes

*Don't forget that steamers (that is, clams with soft shells that are conducive to steaming) are seasonal, as are other types of shell-fish.*

**2 lb steamers**
**1/4 cup beer or dry white wine**
**1/4 cup water**
**8 cloves garlic**
**8 sprigs parsley**
**2 tbsp butter**
**handful freshly ground black pepper**

1. The steamers should be relatively clean, but to be on the safe side, rinse them under cold water and remove any beards of seaweed sticking out from the shells.

2. Dump them into a large stockpot with all the remaining ingredients, set them on the stove over a high flame and bring to a boil. As soon as the liquid boils, the steamers should start to open; once they're all open, remove them from the stockpot with a large slotted spoon and put them in a bowl. Toss away any that have not opened (bad clams).

3. Strain the steaming liquid through a paper towel-lined colander into another bowl, then put both bowls on the table.

4. For those of you not in the know, you eat a steamer like this: Remove the clam from its shell, then peel away the black membrane on its long, skinny end. Dip the clam into the steaming liquid and wriggle it around a couple of times to remove any bits of sand or grit. Then, pop it in your mouth, chew, and swallow.

# Boiled Lobster the Traditional Way

    1 hour

**2 lobsters, at least 1 lb each**
**1/2 cup butter (optional)**

1. Bring a large stockpot of water to a boil. Add the lobsters, one at a time, headfirst, pushing them into the hot water with a big spoon so they die quickly. Cook 10-20 minutes (10 minutes a pound, usually), until nicely reddened all over.

2. If you care to sully your lobster with butter, melt it while the lobsters are cooking in a small saucepot over a very low flame. Place it in bowls, and use for dipping.

# Boiled Lobsters the Fragrant Way

   1 hour

**2 lobsters**
**1 stick cinnamon**
**8 cloves**
**6 star anise**
**10 whole black peppercorns**
**peel of 1 lemon**

1. Follow directions for Boiled Lobster the Traditional Way above, only add all the above ingredients (minus the lobster, of course) to the water before you put it on to boil.

# Mussels Over Linguini

    **30 minutes**

**1 lb mussels**
**1 recipe Spicy Tomato Sauce (p. 101)**
**1/2 lb linguini**

1. Mussels require much scrubbing. Wash them well with a brush under cold running water and yank out their pesky seaweed beards. Set aside in a colander. Refrigerate until ready to use.

2. Cook the linguini according to spaghetti directions on p. 92.

3. About 5 minutes before spicy tomato sauce is cooked, add the mussels, then cover the pot with a lid. All the shells should be open after cooking; discard any mussels that are still closed before serving the sauce—shells and all (pick the mussels out as you go and have a big bowl on hand for shell disposal)—over cooked linguini.

# 9

# *Dead Plants: Strictly Vegetarian*

Maybe you really are a vegetarian, or maybe you only have $5.00 left in your supermarket budget for the week, in which case meat is definitely out of the question. Either way, following are meatless meals which'll fill you up and provide crucial nourishment. We've also included a bunch of vegetable side dishes here, mostly because we didn't know where else to put them.

## Perfect Rice Every Time

Perfect rice is within your grasp, even if you aren't lucky enough to have one of those fancy electric gadgets. Forget what they tell you on the box: rice made the way they instruct always winds up burning on us. The trick is extra water.

For 1 cup cooked rice (serves 2 people): bring 1 1/4 cups water to boil in heavy-bottomed, medium sauce pot. Add 1/2 tsp salt, 1 tbsp butter or margarine, 1/2 cup rice, and stir quickly. Reduce heat as low as it will go, cover pot, and cook 20 minutes. If it's not perfect, don't blame us: you're obviously doing something wrong.

# Vegetarian Main Dishes
# Vegetable Curry

    1 hour

| | |
|---|---|
| 3/4 head cauliflower | 1/2 cup dried lentils |
| 1 cup water | 3 tbsp oil |
| 1 medium onion | 2 cloves garlic |
| 1/2 tsp salt | 1/2 tsp black |
| 2 tbsp curry powder | pepper |
| 1/2 tsp turmeric | 1/4 tsp cayenne |
| (optional) | pepper |
| 1 tsp ground coriander | 2 carrots |
| 4 tbsp tomato juice, | 1 cup cooked rice |
| or 2 tbsp tomato paste | (see left) |

1. Remove the stem from the cauliflower and cut the head into florets. Peel and chop the carrots.

2. Peel and chop the onion. Chop the garlic.

3. Heat the oil in a large skillet over a medium flame and add the onion and garlic; cook 1 minute, stirring often. Add garlic and cook an additional minute.

4. Add the cauliflower, carrots, tomato juice or paste, and spices, and stir to mix. Add the lentils and water and stir well. Reduce flame to low, cover skillet, and cook 30-40 minutes, stirring occasionally to make sure nothing's sticking, until lentils are tender and all the water is evaporated.

5. Serve with rice.

*Add 1/4 cup chopped cilantro, leaves only, at the end of step 4.*

*Serve over basmati rice.*

# Red Beans and Rice

    30 minutes

**15-oz can red kidney beans**
**2 tbsp oil**
**1 clove garlic**
**1 small onion**
**1/4 tsp salt**
**1/2 tsp black pepper**
**4 or more dashes Tabasco**
**2 tsp dried oregano**
**1/2 can water**
**1/2 vegetable bouillon cube (optional)**
**1 cup cooked rice (p. 156)**

1. Chop the onion and set aside.

2. Smash the garlic, remove skin, and set aside.

3. Open beans with a can opener.

4. In a medium saucepot, heat the oil over a medium flame, add the onion and cook 2 minutes, stirring occasionally; add the garlic and cook 1 more minute, stirring constantly to prevent it from browning.

5. Add beans and 1/2 can water, 1/2 bouillon cube, and the spices. Bring to a boil, then reduce flame to low and cover the pot. Cook 20-25 minutes, until mixture has thickened. Serve over cooked rice.

## Don't Buy Those Dried Beans

Tempted to buy those dried beans that look so cheerful in their bins all in a row at the specialty store? Forget about it. Dried beans require soaking—usually overnight in order to soften them up and release their natural, gas-inducing toxins. Even the quick soaking method, which requires boiling them for 2 minutes, then letting them soak an hour before cooking (up to 2 hours), is not nearly as quick as opening up a can of Goya and dumping its contents into a pot. Do it this way or suffer the consequences.

# Black Beans and Rice

      30 minutes

**15-oz can black beans**
**2 tbsp oil**
**1 small red onion**
**1 clove garlic**
**2 capfuls vinegar**
**3/4 tbsp cumin**
**1 tsp ground coriander**
**1/4 tsp salt**
**1/4 tsp black pepper**
**3 capfuls vinegar**
**4 or more dashes Tabasco**
**1/2 can water**
**1 cup cooked rice (p. 156)**

1. Follow steps 1-4 Red Beans and Rice (p. 157).
2. Add beans to pot with vinegar, water, spices, pepper and salt, and Tabasco. Stir, bring to a boil, then reduce flame to low, and cook approximately 20 minutes, until beans are goopy. Serve over rice.

*Add 1/2 can beer instead of water.*

*Add 1 tbsp chopped fresh coriander with spices.*

# Stir-Fry

   30 minutes

**1 small head broccoli**
**1 medium zucchini**
**1 red pepper**
**2 cloves garlic,**
   **chopped**
**4 tbsp oil**
**2 tbsp soy sauce**
**1 tsp black pepper**
**1 cup cooked rice (p. 156)**

1. Wash broccoli, remove stem, and cut into florets.

2. Wash zucchini, cut in half widthwise, then cut into 1/2-inch strips.

3. Wash the red pepper; cut in half lengthwise, remove seed core and stem, and cut into 1/2-inch strips.

4. In a large skillet or wok, heat the oil over medium-high flame. Add broccoli, garlic, and black pepper and cook 2 minutes, stirring constantly.

5. Add zucchini and 1 tbsp soy sauce; cook 2 more minutes, stirring constantly.

6. Add peppers and remaining soy sauce. Cook 1 minute, remove from heat, serve over rice

*Add 1 tbsp fresh grated ginger in step 4.*

*Substitute 1 tbsp sesame oil for 1 tbsp regular oil.*

*Add 1/4 cup sliced drained water chestnuts with zucchini.*

## Not Mississippi Masala

Garam masala is a mixture of aromatic spices that's used frequently in Indian cooking. If you can't find a jar at the health or specialty store, mix up a batch yourself by grinding together the following ingredients in a coffee grinder: 1 tbsp cardamon seed, 1 tsp peppercorns, 1/3 nutmeg pod, 1 tsp cloves, 1 inch of cinnamon stick, and 1 tsp cumin seed.

(Source: *Madhur Jaffrey's Spice Kitchen*)

# Middle Eastern Thing

*This dish gets better with age. Make it a day ahead and reheat in a covered pot over a very low flame.*

    **25 minutes**

**15-oz can chickpeas, drained and rinsed**
**28-oz can whole tomatoes, drained**
**6 cloves garlic, chopped**
**2 medium onions, chopped**
**2 tbsp oil**
**1 tbsp garam masala (see left)**
**1 tsp ground chana masala (optional)**
**1 cup cooked rice (p. 156)**

1.  Heat the oil in a large skillet over medium flame, add the onion, and cook 1 minute. Add garlic and cook, stirring often, until onion is translucent.

2.  Add the remaining ingredients. Stir to incorporate, and cut tomatoes into small pieces with the back of the spoon. Cook approximately 10 minutes, until well heated through. Remove from heat and serve over rice.

# Lentils and Rice

   1 hour

**1 cup dried lentils, rinsed**
**1 medium yellow onion, chopped**
**2 tbsp oil**
**3 cups water + 2 vegetable bouillon cubes**
**1/4 tsp black pepper**
**large pinch ground coriander**
**large pinch garlic powder**
**1 cup cooked rice (p. 156)**

1. Heat the oil in a large skillet over medium flame, add onion, and cook 2-3 minutes, until translucent.

2. Add remaining ingredients (minus rice), stir and bring to a boil.

3. Reduce flame to low and cover pot. Cook 30-40 minutes, until lentils are tender and most of the water is evaporated. Serve over rice.

 *Add 1 diced carrot with the onion and 1/4 cup additional water with lentils.*

## We're Cuckoo for Couscous

Couscous is, after all, just another grain and we're not quite sure what all the fuss is about. However, it does provide a nice texture change from boiled rice. To make 2 servings: Boil 1 cup water with 1 tsp salt and 1 tbsp butter; add 1/2 cup couscous, stir quickly, turn off flame, and cover. Let sit for about 5 minutes, until all the water is absorbed. Uncover pot and fluff up with a fork.

# Ratatouille

     **1-1/2 hours**

| | |
|---|---|
| 2 medium zucchini | 1 small eggplant |
| 3 medium tomatoes | 1 small onion |
| 2 cloves garlic | 1 bay leaf |
| 2 tbsp olive oil | 1 tsp + 1/2 tsp salt |
| 1/2 tsp black pepper | 1/2 tsp red pepper flakes |
| 1 cup water | pinch of sugar |
| 1 cup dry red or white wine | 1 cup cooked couscous (see left) |

1. Remove the stem from the eggplant, then cut eggplant into 1-inch pieces. Place in a colander in the sink, sprinkle with 1 tsp salt (make sure you cover it on both sides), and allow to sit while you cut up the rest of the vegetables.

2. Wash the zucchini, cut them in half lengthwise, then into 1-inch half-moons. Set aside.

3. Wash the tomatoes, core them, and chop. Set aside.

4. Smash the garlic cloves and remove the skin. Set aside.

5. Chop the onion and set aside.

6. Heat the oil in a large skillet over medium heat, add the onion, and cook 2 minutes. Add the garlic and cook 2 more minutes, stirring constantly.

7. Add the tomatoes with 1/2 tsp salt, bay leaf, and pinch of sugar and cook 10 minutes, stirring often.

8. Wipe off the eggplant with a paper towel and add to the skillet; cook 5 minutes, then add zucchini, pepper, wine, water, and red pepper flakes. Reduce flame to medium-low and cook 1 hour, stirring occasionally, until vegetables are tender and tomatoes have reduced to a thick sauce. Serve over couscous.

# Ford's Burritos

*They're relatively easy, they're delicious, they're filling; the only problem is that they require a lot of bowls. Make them anyway.*

   **30 minutes**

**4 flour tortillas**
**1 cup refried beans**
**1 large tomato**
**2 cups fresh spinach**
**1/3 recipe guacamole (p. 187)**
**1 cup jarred or fresh salsa (p. 188)**
**1/2 cup sour cream**
**1/4 cup canned jalapeños**
**6 sprigs fresh coriander, leaves only**

1. Preheat the oven to 200°F.

2. Wash the tomato, core it, and chop fine. Place in a bowl.

3. Wash the spinach, drain it, pat it dry with a paper towel, and place in a bowl.

4. Place the guacamole, salsa, sour cream, jalapeños, and coriander in separate bowls. Then put all of the bowls on the table.

5. Place the tortillas in the oven to warm (about 5 minutes), then put them on plates. Put the refried beans in a skillet and heat over medium heat (2-4 minutes); remove from heat and place in a bowl.

   **To eat:** Place spoonfuls of all the ingredients in the center of a tortilla, roll it up, and cram it into your mouth. Yummy!

## Deviled Potatoes

"When introduced to Europe, the potato was considered an evil food. The Scots refused to eat it because it wasn't mentioned in the Bible. Leprosy, consumption, and rickets were attributed to potato eating."

from Robert E. Rhoades, *National Geographic*, May 1982

"Pass the Peas,"
by James Brown

"Nutrition," by
The Dead Milkmen

# Vegetable Side Dishes

We admit we're getting a little exotic in this section, but don't worry; the hardest thing about these recipes is finding some of the ingredients.

# Baked Acorn Squash

   **1 hour and 15 minutes**

**1 acorn squash, approximately the size of a small dog's head**
**2 tbsp brown sugar**
**1 tbsp raisins (optional)**
**salt and black pepper**
**1 tbsp butter or margarine**

1. Preheat oven to 350°F.

2. With a large, sharp knife, cut the squash in half lengthwise; scoop out the seeds with a spoon and place, shell-side down, in an ovenproof dish.

3. Sprinkle the squash cavities with salt and pepper; put 1 tbsp brown sugar and 1/2 tbsp raisins (if desired) in the cavity of each squash half and top with 1/2 tbsp butter.

4. Place squash in oven, and cook about 1 hour, until tender.

# Sweet and Sour Zucchini

    15 minutes

 *The Classic Vegetable Cookbook,* by Ruth Spear

 *The Savory Way,* by Deborah Madison with Edward Espe Brown

2 small zucchini
2 cloves garlic
1-1/2 tbsp olive oil
1/4 tsp salt
1/4 tsp black pepper
2 capfuls vinegar (preferably balsamic; add
   pinch of sugar if using red wine vinegar)

1. Wash the zucchini and trim off the ends. Slice them in half lengthwise, then cut widthwise into 1-inch pieces. Set aside.

2. Smash the garlic cloves under the flat side of a knife and remove the skin. Set aside.

3. Heat the oil in a heavy-bottomed skillet over medium flame; add the zucchini and garlic, salt and pepper, and cook, stirring often, until zucchini begins to brown, 5-7 minutes. Add the vinegar (and sugar, if using red wine vinegar) and stir to incorporate. Cook an additional 30 seconds, until the zucchini is coated with the vinegar. Remove from flame and serve.

egg versus eggplant

# Stuffed Artichokes

   **60 minutes**

**2 medium-sized artichokes**
**1/2 cup breadcrumbs**
**1 clove garlic**
**2 to 3 pinches salt**
**1/4 tsp black pepper**
**2 tbsp olive oil**

1. Cut the stems off the artichokes so that they can sit straight up; cut the tips off the leaves (about 1 inch). Set aside.

2. Place the breadcrumbs in a bowl with the salt and pepper; crush the garlic cloves with a garlic press and add to the breadcrumbs with the oil. Stir with a fork to make a paste.

3. To stuff the artichokes, pull apart the leaves as far as they'll go and spoon equal amounts of the breadcrumb mixture into them. Place in a small stockpot that has 1/2 to 1 inch of water at the bottom, cover, and set over a medium-low flame. Bring to a boil, then reduce flame to low. Cook 30-45 minutes, until leaves pull easily away from the stalk.

# Parsleyed Potatoes

   30 minutes

**1 lb potatoes**
**1 tbsp butter or margarine**
**2 pinches of salt**
**1/4 tsp black pepper**
**2 tbsp chopped parsley, leaves only**

1. Wash the potatoes, cut them into 2-inch pieces and place in a medium saucepot. Cover with cold water and bring to a boil over high flame. Reduce flame to medium and cook 15-20 minutes, until tender.

2. Drain the potatoes into a colander and place back in pot. Add butter, salt, pepper, and parsley and mix well until butter is melted. Serve immediately.

*Add juice of 1/4 lemon in step 2.*

*The Greens Cookbook*, by Deborah Madison with Edward Espe Brown

*Madhur Jaffrey's World-of-the-East Vegetarian Cookbook*

# Glazed Carrots

   **30 minutes**

**4 medium-sized carrots**
**2 tbsp butter or margarine**
**1/2 cup water**
**1-1/2 tsp sugar**
**1/4 tsp salt**
**1/4 tsp black pepper**

1. Peel the carrots, trim off the ends, and cut into thin rounds. Place in skillet with remaining ingredients and bring to a boil. Lower flame to medium and cook, stirring often, for 15-20 minutes, until carrots are tender and all the liquid has cooked off.

# Asparagus in Mustard Vinaigrette

   **30 minutes**

**1 bunch asparagus**
**1 recipe mustard dressing (p. 84)**

1. Cut about 1/2 inch from the thick ends of the asparagus. Wash, and place in a large skillet with water to cover the bottom. Cook over medium-high heat for 10-15 minutes, until tender. Drain into a colander and run under cold water to cool. Divide evenly between two plates and top with vinaigrette.

# Fava Beans with Tomatoes and Garlic

30 minutes

1-1/2 to 2 lbs fava beans
2 tbsp olive oil
2 small fresh tomatoes or 3 canned tomatoes, chopped
2 cloves garlic, chopped
1/4 tsp + pinch salt
1/4 tsp black pepper

1. Crack open the fava shells, remove the beans, and place in a medium saucepot with a pinch of salt. Cover with water and cook over medium flame until tender, about 15 minutes.

2. Drain the beans in a colander and return to pot with remaining ingredients. Cook over medium flame, stirring often, until tomato liquid has evaporated, 5-7 minutes. Serve.

*Bean Banquets,*
by Patricia Gregory

*James McNair's
Potato Cookbook*

*The Enchanted
Broccoli Forest,*
by Mollie Katzen

# Sautéed Wild Mushrooms

   **20 minutes**

**1/2 lb wild mushrooms**
**(like portobello, shitake, chanterelle)**
**2 tbsp butter or margarine**
**2 tbsp olive oil**
**2 tbsp chopped garlic or shallots**
**1 tbsp balsamic vinegar**
**1/2 tsp salt**
**1/2 tsp black pepper**

1. Wipe the dirt off the mushrooms with a paper towel and trim off the tips of the stems. Cut the mushrooms into 1/2-inch slices.

2. Heat the butter and oil in a medium skillet over medium flame and add the mushrooms and remaining ingredients minus the vinegar. Stirring often, cook for approximately 5-7 minutes, until mushrooms are wilted. Add vinegar, stir, and cook an additional 45 seconds.

3. Remove mushrooms from pan with a slotted spoon and divide evenly between two plates.

*Place cooked mushrooms on arugala leaves and top with grated Parmesan cheese.*

# Corn Relish

   1 hour and 15 minutes

8-3/4-oz can corn, drained
1/2 15-oz can black
   beans, rinsed       2 tsp olive oil
   and drained        1/4 tsp salt
1 small red pepper,
   chopped
1 tsp balsamic vinegar
1/4 tsp black pepper

1. Mix all the ingredients together in a small bowl. Cover and chill for 1 hour before serving.

# Braised Red Cabbage

   30 minutes

1 small red cabbage     2 tbsp oil
1/2 cup red wine        1/2 tsp salt
1/2 tsp black pepper    1 tbsp brown sugar
1 Granny Smith apple

1. Slice the cabbage by cutting it in half lengthwise, removing the core, and chopping into strips. Set aside.

2. Heat the oil in a large skillet over high flame and add the cabbage, salt, pepper, and sugar. Stir, reduce flame to medium-low, and cover.

3. Quarter the apple, peel and dice. Set aside.

4. Stir cabbage occasionally; after 10 minutes, add red wine, increase flame to medium, stir, and cook, uncovered, an additional 5 minutes. Add diced apple, and cook an additional 5–7 minutes, until cabbage is tender and the liquid is evaporated. Serve immediately.

# 10

## Is that Dessert, or Are You Just Glad to See Me?

We don't think a meal is complete until we've consumed something containing sugar. This usually means that after dinner, we're so stuffed and bloated that we can only muster enough energy to roll ourselves from the table to the couch. But, as it happens, this works out just fine. The couch is soft and cozy, the remote is within arm's reach, and *Seinfeld* is in nightly syndication. No reason to move again until bedtime.

## Marangue -vs- Merengue

Confused? So were we, once. Let us disentangle your brain: Marangue is sweetened, whipped egg whites, frequently used to top, say, lemon marangue pie, or baked and used as a receptacle for custard or poached fruit. The merengue, according to *The Random House Dictionary of the English Language*, is a "ballroom dance of Dominican and Haitian origin, characterized by a stiff-legged, limping step." Not to be confused with the Spanish meaning of the word: "A sickly person; invalid."

# Baked Apples

   **1 hour**

**2 large apples, preferably Rome**
**2 tbsp brown sugar**
**1 tsp cinnamon**
**1 tbsp unsalted butter**

1. Preheat oven to 350°F.

2. Remove the seeds and stems of the apples with an apple corer. Place in a small baking dish, and fill dish with an inch of water.

3. Mix together the sugar and cinnamon and spoon into hollow centers of the apples. Top each one with 1/2 tbsp butter.

4. Place apples on center rack of oven and bake 30-45 minutes, until soft. Eat immediately with spoons.

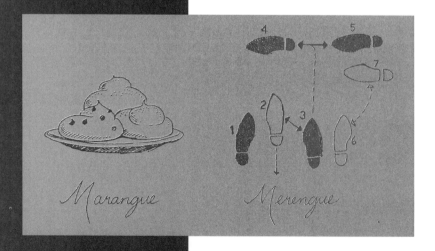

*Marangue*          *Merengue*

# Apple Tart

   1 hour

**2 apples, preferably Granny Smith**
**1 sheet frozen puff pastry**
**flour**
**1 tbsp sugar**
**1/2 tsp cinnamon**
**2 tbsp unsalted butter or margarine**

1.  Preheat oven to 400°F.
2.  Allow puff pastry to thaw for 5 minutes, then sprinkle flour on flat, dry surface, place pastry on it, and roll to about 1/8 of an inch with a rolling pin or large glass bottle. Place on a cookie sheet.
3.  Quarter the apples, peel them, then cut into very thin slices. Arrange in slightly overlapping pattern on top of the puff pastry, leaving an inch border around the edges.
4.  Mix together the cinnamon and sugar, then sprinkle over apples. Dot with butter. Place on center rack of oven and bake 30-35 minutes, until puff pastry is golden.
5.  Serve immediately with ice cream or wrap and store in the fridge and eat cold for breakfast.

# Poached Pears in Wine Syrup

     **30 minutes**

**2 ripe pears**
**1 lemon**
**1/2 cup red wine**
**1/8 cup sugar**

1. Quarter the pears, peel them, and place them in a large skillet. Squeeze lemon juice over them and mix well.

2. Add wine and sugar to the pears, then place over medium-high flame and bring to a boil. Cook, stirring often, for 10-15 minutes, until wine has thickened to a syrup. Remove from flame and divide evenly between two plates.

 *Add 2 tsp fresh grated ginger at beginning step 2.*

 *Serve with fresh whipped cream.*

# Banana Bread

*Here's an economical way to dispose of those brown bananas.*

    **1 hour and 30 minutes**

**3 extremely ripe bananas**
**1/2 cup + 1 tbsp unsalted butter or margarine**
**1 cup sugar**

**2 eggs**
**1-3/4 cups flour**
**pinch of salt**
**2 tsp baking soda**
**1/4 cup milk**

1. Preheat oven to 350°F.

2. Peel bananas and, in a large bowl, mash them with a fork. Set aside.

3. Break the eggs into a separate bowl and beat them. Set aside.

4. In another bowl, sift together the flour, salt, and baking soda.

5. Yes, one more bowl, this time for 1/2 cup of the butter and the sugar: With a hand mixer—or a fork if you don't have a hand mixer—cream together the butter and sugar (that means, whip it up until it's homogenous). Add the eggs and beat until the mixture is fluffy.

6. Add the flour mixture, a handful at a time, and mix well to combine.

7. Add the milk to the batter and mix well to combine.

8. Add the bananas and mix well.

9. Butter a 6-1/2 x 10-1/2 inch loaf pan with the remaining tbsp butter, and add batter. Place on center rack of oven and bake 50-55 minutes, until a toothpick or small knife inserted into the center of the loaf comes out clean. Remove the bread from the pan and allow to cool on a rack. Wrap in tin foil and store in or out of the refrigerator.

### How Twinkies Are Made

**It's quite possible that you have enjoyed twinkies in the past and maybe continue to do so today. If so, just remember: there is no baking involved in the manufacture of a twinkie. They're just sort of sprayed into a mold and left to set. Pretty sobering, eh?**

### The Twinkie Defense

**In 1978, San Francisco Supervisor Dan White shot and killed fellow Supervisor Harvey Milk and Mayor George Moscone. At his trial, White claimed his actions were due to his having eaten too many Twinkies that morning.**

# Peanut Butter Cookies

**2** **25 minutes**

**3/4 cup sugar**
**3 egg whites**
**1 cup peanut butter**
**1/2 tsp salt**
**1 tbsp unsalted butter or margarine**

1. Preheat oven to 350°F.
2. Separate the eggs by cracking in half over a bowl and juggling yolk back and forth between two shell halves. Discard yolks and shells. Beat the egg whites with a hand mixer—use a medium-sized whisk if you don't have a mixer—until they're stiff. Add the sugar and beat until well incorporated. Add the salt and peanut butter, and mix well to combine.
3. Grease two cookie sheets with the butter and drop the batter, 1 tsp at a time, onto them. (If you have only one cookie sheet, bake one batch, then repeat this step after you've taken them out of the oven.) Leave at least 1 inch of space between cookies. Place the sheets on the center rack of the oven and bake 10-12 minutes, until cookies are just set and are slightly brown around the edges.

# Bread Pudding

   1 hour

**2 cups tightly packed stale bread, cut into 1-inch pieces**
**1 tbsp unsalted butter or margarine**
**2 eggs**
**1 cup milk**
**1/2 tsp vanilla**
**1/4 cup + 1/4 cup sugar**
**1 tsp cinnamon**

1. Preheat oven to 375°F.

2. Grease an oven proof dish with the butter. Add bread.

3. Put the milk in a medium saucepot and heat over medium flame until it begins to bubble. In the meantime, in a medium bowl, beat the eggs until they turn a light yellow color (hand mixer works best), then add 1/4 cup of the sugar and vanilla, and mix well to incorporate. Whisking constantly, add the hot milk in a steady stream. Pour over bread.

4. Mix together the cinnamon and remaining 1/4 cup sugar and sprinkle over bread mixture. Place dish in another large, ovenproof dish, add hot water so that it reaches halfway up the inside dish, and place in oven. Bake approximately 40 minutes, until the custard has set. Remove from oven and eat while it's hot.

## Twinkie Cake

"When I lived in Williamsburgh, Brooklyn, I had this New Year's Eve dinner. This was in the days when all you could get in the neighborhood was cauliflower, Goya beans, and vodka. I was going to make an angel food ice-box cake, but I hadn't been able to find angel food any-where. I was so desperate that I went into the local bodega and bought 50 Twinkies. There was this motorcycle guy in there and he was like, "You got a serious case of the munchies, huh?" I brought the Twinkies home and made the cake with them. A friend was bringing her cousin from Paris and she said, "My cousin is really a snob; I'm sorry in advance if she doesn't like any-thing." I gave her the Twinkie cake and she kept asking for more. Everyone thought I was drunk because I couldn't stop laughing. That was the best I ever made that cake."

Margo G.,
Brown University

"Smokin' Banana Peels," by the Dead Milkmen

 "Brown Sugar," by the Stones

 "Chocolate City," by Parliament

 "Sweetest Pie," by Curve

 "Ice Cream Man," by Jonathan Richmond

 "Savoy Truffle," by The Beatles

# Fancy Fruit Salad

  1-1/2 hours

**1 pint blueberries**
**1 pint raspberries or strawberries**

**Any 3 of the following:**
   **2 kiwis, sliced**
   **1 mango, peeled and chopped**
   **1 papaya peeled, seeded and chopped**
   **4 figs, stemmed and quartered**
   **1/2 cup cubed melon (not watermelon)**
   **1/2 cup champagne grapes, stalks removed**

**juice of 4 oranges**
**juice of 1 lemon**
**2 tbsp sherry**
**2 tsp fresh grated ginger**
**1 tbsp sugar**

1. Place all the fruit in a large bowl.

2. Mix the orange and lemon juices, the sherry, sugar, and ginger in a smaller bowl. Pour over fruit; cover the bowl with plastic wrap, and place in refrigerator for 1 hour before serving.

 *Add 2 tbsp fresh, chopped mint before putting in fridge.*

## Ice Cream Toppings

Nothing in the cabinets that can be translated into a baked good? Buy a pint of your favorite ice cream, and try one of these toppings:

1. **Chocolate sauce:** Place a regular-sized Hershey bar in a small glass or stainless steel bowl; add 3 tbsp butter, and place over a pot of simmering—not boiling—water. Stir constantly until chocolate has melted, and don't get any water in it or it'll turn lumpy.

2. **Berries in syrup:** Put 1/2 cup frozen berries in a saucepot with 1/4 cup sugar, 2 tbsp water, and 2 tbsp cognac, bourbon, or sherry. Place on stove over medium heat, stirring constantly, and cook 7-10 minutes, until syrupy.

3. **With candied nuts:** Put 1/2 cup nuts of your choice in a small, heavy-bottomed skillet with 1/4 cup sugar. Place on stove over high heat and cook, stirring constantly, until sugar has melted, browned, and turned to hard caramel. Eat instantly, or it will turn to brittle.

## Dolomite?

How does Hershey's get its chocolate so rich and creamy? Rocks. That's right, the Hershey Company is one of America's largest consumers of dolomite, a form of limestone, which they use, in powdered form, as an emulsifier.

# Apple Pie

   **1 hour and 30 minutes**

**2 deep-dish frozen pie shells**
**6 apples, preferably Granny Smith**
**1 lemon**
**1/3 cup sugar**
**1/3 cup brown sugar**
**1-1/2 tsp cinnamon**
**2 tbsp unsalted butter or margarine**

1. Remove the pie shells from the freezer and preheat the oven to 400°F.

2. Quarter the apples, core and peel them, and cut each quarter into 4 more slices. Place in a bowl and squeeze lemon juice over them. Mix well with your hands.

3. Mix the sugars and cinnamon together in a bowl.

4. Place half the apples in one of the pie shells. Sprinkle with half the cinnamon sugar; top with remaining apples, sprinkle with remaining cinnamon sugar, then dot with butter.

5. Remove the second pie shell from its pan, flatten on a cutting board, then place over apples. Pinch the two shells together with your fingers, then trim off the excess around the edges. Cut 4 or 5 slits into the top of the pie shell with a sharp knife, then place the pie on the center rack of the oven. Bake 55 minutes to 1 hour, until top crust is nicely golden. Excellent when served warm with ice cream.

# 11

# *The Gang's All Here: Entertaining*

## Inviting Over Everyone You Know

Don't you just love entertaining friends? They bring over a forty of Olde English, drink your reserves of Heineken, and break the toilet and glassware. Why bother entertaining at all? Because eventually they'll be forced to reciprocate. If days later you're still finding plastic beer cups behind the sofa, on the top shelf of the closet, wedged between the bed and the dresser, your party was a big success.

## Microbrews

According to an article in *The Washingtonian* (August 1994), microbrews are:

1. Made by small companies in small batches.

2. Unpasteurized and preservative-free, which means they can't be shipped very far.

3. Made just with barley, as opposed to traditional American beers, which are made from a combination of barley, corn, and rice.

Yes, your apartment will be trashed afterwards, but there's something deeply satisfying about cramming 100 people into a room the size of a Buick. If you do things right, they'll all be too giddy from beer consumption to realize they're uncomfortable.

For a party like this, invest in a beer ball or a keg. A ball will inebriate about ten people, a keg, up to forty. And even if you don't know how to tap it, chances are you've invited someone who does. Buy twice as many big plastic cups as you think you'll need (as the night wears on, cups will mysteriously disappear, only to reappear as soggy ashtrays), and lots of snacks (you don't want anyone getting sick on your nice linoleum). Chips and pretzels are good, so are various dips, like the ones that follow.

# Guacamole

   20 minutes

*Serves 20 (hopefully)*

**6 very ripe avocados**
**6 tbsp chopped fresh cilantro**
**3 limes**
**4 tbsp oil**
**6 cloves garlic**
**4 tsp salt, or more to taste**
**3 tsp black pepper, or more to taste**
**1-1/2 tsp (mild) or 3 tsp (hot) Tabasco**
**1-1/2 tsp ground coriander**

1. Cut the avocados in half; remove the pits, then scoop the flesh into a large bowl with a spoon.

2. Cut limes in half and squeeze juice into avocados. Add oil. Put garlic cloves in garlic press and squeeze into avocados. Add salt, Tabasco, and spices, and mash the whole thing together with a fork. Add the cilantro and mix well.

 *Add 1 cup chopped tomatoes, 1/2 cup chopped red onion, and/or 1/4 cup chopped jalapeños.*

*Great Wine Values, The Wine Spectator*, and *The Bartender's Guide*

"Spill the Wine," by War

"Love Hangover," by Diana Ross

# Salsa

   **1-1/2 hours**

*Serves 20*

**15 ripe tomatoes**
**1/2 cup cilantro, leaves only, chopped**
**1 large red onion, chopped**
**6 cloves garlic, chopped**
**4 fresh jalapeños, seeded and chopped**
**juice of 3 limes**
**4 tbsp oil**
**1 tsp salt**
**1/2 tsp black pepper**
**1 tsp Tabasco**
**1/4 tsp cayenne pepper**
**1 tsp ground coriander**
**2 tsp red wine vinegar**
**1/2 tsp sugar**

1. Wash and core the tomatoes and chop them fine. Place in a large bowl.
2. Add everything else, mix well, wrap, and let sit at room temperature for 1 hour before serving.

 Add 10 tomatillos, removed from their husks and chopped.

*Tomatillo*

*Tomato*

# Hummus

  15 minutes

*Serves 20*

**2 cans chickpeas, drained**
**4 cloves garlic**
**3 tbsp tahini**
**3 tsp salt**
**1/4 cup water**
**2 tbsp olive oil**
**juice of 1-1/2 lemons**
**1 tsp coriander**

1. Place all the ingredients in a blender with the lemon juice. Puree and place in a serving bowl.

All the above dips can be served with tortilla chips or pieces of pita. A final party note: Pick lots of music in advance, and don't let too much time elapse between CDs. Every friend you know who's in a band will show up with a demo tape, and unless you want your guests to clear out early, don't leave the stereo unattended for long.

## Cheap but Potable Wine List

1. **Ravenwood Zinfandel:** Dry and fruity; goes great with all kinds of different food, especially Indian. $9.00 (California)

2. **Montecillo Vina Cumbrero:** Dry and full-bodied; excellent with red meat and heartier pasta dishes. $5.00 (Spain)

3. **Santa Carolina Merlot, Cabernet, Chardonnay:** From $4.00-$6.00 (Chile)

4. **Los Vascos Cabernet:** Full-bodied; drink with typical winter foods. $6.00 (Chile)

# The Cocktail Party

So you think you're a grownup. Well, if you're considering throwing a cocktail party, you must be well on your way. Either that, or you just finished reading *Breakfast at Tiffany's.* Ten is the ideal number of guests, twenty-five is max. Music should be mellower for this kind of event (jazz is perfect, funk is appropriate, too). Buy a few six packs of decent beer—like Bass, Samuel Adams, Becks Dark, Harpoon, Anchor Steam—some potable wine, and a fifth each of gin, vodka, scotch, and bourbon. And don't forget bags of ice and the mixers: O.J., tonic, club soda, Coke (three to four bottles of each), and a bottle of dry vermouth for mixing martinis.

## Glasses

# How to Feed the Cocktail Party

**2 loaves French bread**

**2 boxes crackers**

**3 wedges of cheese such as brie, cheddar, Jarlsberg, Port Salut**

**1/2 lb black olives (spring for the kind with pits that don't come in a can)**

**1 lb cheese sticks**

**mixed nuts**

**cookies**

**fruit, such as grapes and strawberries**

1. Cut up the bread into 1-inch slices and place in a bowl or a basket. Open one box of crackers and put on a plate. Unwrap the cheeses and place on a large plate with a small knife. Place bread, cheese, and crackers on a table, in close proximity to each other.

2. Put some of the olives in a bowl. Ditto with the nuts and cheese sticks. Scatter bowls around the room.

3. Wash the fruit and place it in a bowl. If you're serving grapes, cut up into small, single-serving bunches. Put the cookies on a plate. Disperse.

   Be prepared to replenish bowls and plates of food as the night wears on.

5. Oxford Landing: Reds are light, whites are full-bodied. $6.00 (Australia)

6. La Vielle Ferme Cotes du Vertaux, Cotes du Luberon: Red is dry, earthy; white is light and perfect with summer foods, especially tomatoes. $5.00 (France)

7. Coltibuono Cetamura: Fruity; the classic pizza wine. $6.00 (Italy)

8. Brut Dargent (Sparkling): For special occasions, when you can't bear the thought of spending all that money on real Champagne. $8.00 (France)

# The Perfect Martini

   10 minutes

gin
dry vermouth
ice
6 green olives

1. Fill two martini glasses with ice. Add splash dry vermouth to each glass and let sit for 5 minutes.
2. Dump out ice and vermouth, add 3 green olives to each glass, and fill with gin (which you have kept in the freezer for at least 1 hour).

# The Perfect Bloody Mary

    10 minutes

3 oz vodka
1 cup tomato juice
3 tbsp Worcestershire sauce
4 dashes Tabasco
1 tsp horseradish
juice of 1/2 a lime
2 pinches black pepper
ice

1. Fill two tall glasses halfway with ice.
2. Place vodka, tomato juice, Worcestershire sauce, Tabasco, lime juice, horseradish, and black pepper into a cocktail jigger. Shake well. Pour into glasses over ice. Serve with lime wedge, or stalk of celery.

# They Came to Watch Football and Decided to Stay for Dinner

For watching football, an activity that requires intense concentration and one hand free for holding a beer and the other for throwing things at the TV screen, it's best to serve food that can be eaten quickly and doesn't taste disgusting once it gets cold. Since you're feeding your friends, let them bring their own beer.

**Happy Homebrewing Recipes from Bert**

(http://www.columbia.edu/-mac103/homebrew.html) A fun-loving young scientist shares his recipes for everything from Pale Ale to Chocolate Blackberry Ecstasy.

# Nachos

   **20 minutes**

*Serves 8*

**1 large bag tortilla chips**
**2 16-oz cans refried beans**
**2 cups grated Jack or cheddar cheese**
**4-oz can jalapeños, drained**
**1/4 recipe guacamole (p. 187)**
**1/4 recipe salsa (p. 188), or one jar bought sour cream**

1. Preheat oven to 350°F.
2. Lay out tortilla chips on two baking sheets. Top each with 1 tsp refried beans, one slice jalapeño, and sprinkle all over with cheese.
3. Place baking sheets on center rack of oven and bake, approximately 5 minutes, until cheese is melted. Serve with guacamole, salsa, and sour cream—in separate bowls—for dipping.

# Chili

      1 hour and 30 minutes

*Serves 8*

2 large onions
6 cloves garlic
3 tbsp oil
2 lbs ground beef
2 28-oz cans crushed tomatoes
2 15-oz cans red kidney beans, rinsed and
    drained
3 tbsp dried oregano
2-1/2 tbsp cumin
2 tsp coriander
10 cloves
1 tbsp hot chili powder
4 fresh hot peppers, like jalapeños or cayenne
1/2 tsp allspice
2 tsp salt
1 cup beer

1. Chop the onions (p. 43) and smash the garlic to remove the skin. Cut the hot peppers in half, remove the seed core, and remember not to touch your fingers to your eyes. Open the cans of tomatoes, and unwrap the beef.

2. In a large stockpot, heat the oil over medium flame and add the onion; cook 3 minutes then add the garlic and cook an additional 2 minutes, stirring constantly to prevent browning.

3. Add the beef and stir well to break up the pieces. When the beef is browned all over, drain the fat from it and add the tomatoes, peppers, beer, and all the spices. Bring to a boil, then reduce the flame to low, cover the pot, and cook 1 hour, stirring often to make sure nothing's sticking. Add more beer, a splash at a time, if liquid looks too low.

4. Add the beans, re-cover pot, and cook an additional 15 minutes. Serve over rice (p. 156), remembering to quadruple the recipe.

# You and Your Roommate Both Want the Apartment

You've got a date and so does your roommate. And, horror of horrors, you both want the apartment. This could easily come to blows; instead, commit to the unpleasant prospect of having dinner together, all four of you, and agree that afterwards, you'll section off the apartment and avoid each other for the rest of the night.

# Stress-free Lasagna

   **1-1/2 hours**

*For this to be a truly stress-free dish, prepare the lasagna a day in advance, let cool before covering with tin foil and storing in the refrigerator. To heat up, preheat oven to 250°F, place covered lasagna on center rack, and allow to cook 15-20 minutes, until warmed through. Serve with a side salad and a nice bottle of wine.*

**1 tbsp butter or margarine**
**12 lasagna noodles**
**32-oz jar spaghetti sauce**
**16-oz package grated mozzarella**
**16-oz container ricotta cheese**
**1 tbsp grated Parmesan cheese**

1. Preheat oven to 350°F.

2. Cook lasagna noodles as directed on the package; drain, and lay flat on paper towels, to remove excess moisture.

3. Grease the bottom and sides of a 9 x 12 inch rectangular baking pan (or disposable aluminum) with the butter or margarine.

4. Open the jar of spaghetti sauce and spread 4 tbsp on the bottom of the pan.

5. Over the sauce, lie 3 lasagna noodles side-by-side.

6. Spread noodles with 1/3 container ricotta (easiest with your fingers; make sure they're clean, especially if you've been riding the subway); sprinkle with 1/3 package mozzarella; top with 1/2 cup spaghetti sauce, or more if you like it wet.

7. Repeat steps 4 and 5 two more times.

8. Top with 3 more lasagna noodles, and sprinkle with Parmesan.

9. Cover pan with tin foil and place on center rack of oven.

10. Bake 30 minutes, then remove foil and bake an additional 5-10 minutes, enough time for the top to get brown and bubbly, but not long enough for the top noodles to curl up.

# *Index*

# G

garbage bags, 33
garlic, 28
   Broccoli and Garlic Spaghetti, 94-95
   chopping, 44
   Fava Beans with Tomatoes and, 169
   Lemon and Garlic Spaghetti, 93
   powder, 31
   presses, 7
   Tuna with Oil and, 72

ginger, fresh, 36
Glazed Carrots, 168
grapefruit spoons, 14
graters, 7
Grilled Cheese Sandwich, 68
Grilled Tuna Steaks, 146
Guacamole, 187

# H

hamburger
   Complicated, 120
   Standard, 119
   toppings for, 121

hand mixers, 11
hangover remedies, 51, 53
herbs
   dried, 31
   fresh, 35-36, 107

hot dogs, 36
   Split-Fried, 123

hot pots, 11
Hot Sausages with Tomato and Onion, 134
Hummus, 189

# I

ice cream, 38
   toppings for, 181
Italian Dressing, 84
   Tuna with, 72

# J

jar openers, 14
jelly, 28

# K

knives
   chef's, 6
   paring, 8
   sharpeners, 7

# L

ladles, 8
lamb, 38
Lasagna, Stress-Free, 196-197
leftovers
   Chicken Salad, 142
   Chicken Soup from Leftover Baked Chicken, 141
   Chicken Soup with Leftover Spaghetti, 108-109
   Lentil Soup, 65
   Ramen with Leftover Meat, 112
   reheating, 46
   Spaghetti Lo Mein, 108
   Tupperware containers for, 13

lemon(s), 29
   Cutlets, 135

## About the Author

Lela Nargi is a writer who lives in Brooklyn, New York. To supplement her meager writer's income she has worked in catering and on other people's cookbooks, including *Dad Throws a Party* by Bob Sloane. She is a graduate of Bennington College in Vermont.